RADIO ACTIVE

PRAISE FOR *RADIO ACTIVE*

"I found his account riveting, wonderfully written, and exciting to read. He gives the reader a behind the scenes, "Eagle eye" view of personal, historical, and current events that only a handful of people on earth can speak to."
— *Former Congressman Jesse Jackson Jr.*

"I always say love is an action word and Joe Madison has been an example of how acting on words of hope put into actions can change lives for the better."
— *Bebe Winans, singer-songwriter*

"I've known Joe since I was 16 years old. I like his genuineness, humbleness and willingness to hold accountable those who don't fight for the birdies in his nest. You want the Black Eagle on that wall."
— *Donnie Simpson, host of BET's "Video Soul" and Radio Hall of Fame member*

"I honor the relationship I've been privileged to have with the Black Eagle. His commitment to the community and his constant unapologetic free thinking has been a guideline to sparking the minds of many generations. I've learned that he's also a kind and caring person that naturally mentors and provides. Thank you Joe for showing us how it's done!"
— *Sway Calloway, radio personality and host of "Sway in the Morning" on SiriusXM*

"One of my generation's most extraordinary men — in so many dimensions — shares extraordinary (and sometimes jaw-dropping) stories of his life that will inspire and energize you. Joe Madison brings the arc of modern American and world history into bright view through a book filled with adventures and challenges that you won't be able to put down!"
— *Thom Hartmann, talk show host and author of The Hidden History of American Healthcare*

"Buckle up. His memoir is the truth!"
— *Roland S. Martin, #RolandMartinUnfiltered Daily Digital Show*

RADIO ACTIVE

A Memoir of Advocacy in Action,
on the Air and in the Streets

JOE MADISON
with Dave Canton

Copyright © 2021 by Joe Madison.

Library of Congress Control Number: 2018908872
ISBN: Hardcover   978-1-9845-4317-2
              Softcover   978-1-9845-4316-5
              eBook   978-1-9845-4331-8

All rights reserved. No part of this book may be reproduced or transmitted in any form or by any means, electronic or mechanical, including photocopying, recording, or by any information storage and retrieval system, without permission in writing from the copyright owner.

Print information available on the last page.

Rev. date: 09/27/2021

To order additional copies of this book, contact:
Xlibris
844-714-8691
www.Xlibris.com
Orders@Xlibris.com
763436

This book is dedicated to my wife, Sharon LaVerne Madison, who has been my angel on earth.

To my children, Shawna, Jason, Monesha and Michelle, and their children, who inspire me in everything I do and have done for the benefit of their world, and will continue to do until I take my last breath.

Joe Madison

ACKNOWLEDGMENTS

This book is primarily a collaboration between Joe Madison and myself, Dave Canton, but we couldn't have done it without a lot of other people's help.

First among those was our editor, Bryan Monroe, whose unexpected death on Jan. 13, 2021, was a devastating loss to us all. Monroe was an associate professor of journalism at Temple University's Klein College of Media and Communication in Philadelphia. A longtime friend and a frequent guest on Joe's show, Bryan was the former editor of Ebony and Jet and was also assistant vice president of news at Knight Ridder. From 2005 to 2007, he served as president of the National Association of Black Journalists. In 2006, a team of journalists he led won the Pulitzer Prize for Public Service for its coverage of Hurricane Katrina.

Most of this book originated from recorded interviews with Joe and from his radio broadcasts, which I compiled and organized into the current narrative. Bryan, the consummate journalist, played a key role in turning Joe's reminiscences into a fascinating and coherent story.

We would like to thank our final editor, Karl Kahler, designer, Tracy Cox, and copy editor, Debbie Bride, for their contribution to completing this project. We thank our transcribers, Dion Rabouin, Phyllis Greenhill and Christine Fiore, for their excellent work, and Allison Paynter, professor of English at Chaminade University, who edited early portions of the book.

We thank the staff at the Amistad Research Center at Tulane University in New Orleans, where Joe's papers are located. And we thank Connecticut College and the University of Florida, which provided necessary funds to complete the project.

Finally, we would like to thank the Madison family, primarily Joe's wife, Sharon Madison, for their assist in telling this incredible story. We thank Joe's children, Shawna, Monesha, Michelle and Jason, for sharing photos and information about their father.

TABLE OF CONTENTS

Foreword viii

Preface xii

1. Into The War Zone 1
2. Genesis of an Activist 5
3. Who Gave You Permission to Call a Boycott? 27
4. Helluva Place to Do Radio 45
5. Running to Lead the NAACP 53
6. The Sudan Campaign 71
7. My Health Scare 79
8. The Obama Years 86
9. Trump, Obama and the Night it All Began 99
10. The Activist 109
11. It's All Happening So Fast 119
12. A Moment or a Movement 133

FOREWORD

HOOKED ON THE BLACK EAGLE

In 2004, I bought my father an XM satellite radio because he was a San Francisco Giants fan and XM satellite allowed him to listen to every single Giants game on the radio. My father is old-school. He listens to baseball on the radio, does not have an ATM card and is a talk show junkie.

When I called him to see if he had enjoyed XM, he said yes, but he told me that he really enjoyed listening to "The Power" (now called "Urban View"), an all-Black talk station. He told me about "The Black Eagle Show" hosted by Joe Madison from 6 to 10 in the morning. My father is a loyal listener, and he told me one of Joe's famous sayings: "We are culturally conditioned to believe white is better than black, and the manifestation of that condition is to be undervalued, underestimated and marginalized."

Before 2004, I had never heard of Joe Madison. I am a history professor, civil rights scholar and radio talk show fan, but I had never heard of the Black Eagle.

In 2009, I purchased a 2007 Chrysler Town and Country that had satellite radio. When I worked at Connecticut College, I drove an hour to work three to four days a week, so every morning I had the pleasure of listening to the Black Eagle. I was hooked.

Not only did I enjoy listening, I learned a great deal from his show. On some mornings I was so fired up that I brought up Joe's daily discussion topic to my class. When I started listening, Joe asked alumni of historically Black colleges and universities to call their alma mater and ask them to divest from Sudan due to slavery and genocide in Darfur. One morning I sat in my child's middle school parking lot listening to the show and Joe asked his alma mater, Washington University in St. Louis, to divest.

While mainstream media talked about genocide in Darfur, Joe asked his listeners to do something about it. Joe participated in hunger strikes and conducted acts of civil disobedience to protest genocide in Sudan. He traveled to Sudan and did a number of live remotes to give his listeners a view of Sudan from the ground. In 2011, South Sudan became an independent nation. Joe's work paid off.

Joe Madison has been on the radio for more than 40 years, and a great deal has changed for African Americans. In 2003, Oprah Winfrey became the world's first Black female billionaire; in 2008, Barack Obama became the nation's first Black president; and in 2021, Kamala Harris became the first female, Black and Asian vice president.

Yet African Americans remain underrepresented in media, not to mention in corporate boardrooms. This dichotomy of Black progress and structural racism is at the core of the African American experience. But it's Black activism that is the major reason why African Americans have progressed.

When most Americans talk about the civil rights movement, they mention Dr. Martin Luther King Jr. or Rosa Parks. When they talk about the Black Power era, they mention Malcolm X and the Black Panther Party.

However, most civil rights activists were local leaders who will never make the history books. But their stories are engraved in the memories of the thousands of ordinary people they inspired.

Joe's civil rights activism spans 40 years and is a story that is worthy to be told. In addition, Madison has interviewed dozens of civil rights leaders, entertainers and influential African American personalities. Those stories shape the civil rights narrative that Joe will share with you.

Joe has been a voice committed to social justice and this is what separates him from the majority of his contemporaries. He encourages his listeners to become active citizens and not just "armchair" liberals or progressives who suffer from a paralysis of analysis. They can articulate the problems but do not participate in any solutions.

Joe doesn't play that.

Another reason why people tune in to the Black Eagle is that it provides an unapologetic Black perspective. For example, when the media mentions the 6.3 percent unemployment rate, Joe will let you know that the Black unemployment rate is much higher than the national average. If the topic is labor unions, Joe will say he is a union supporter. But he will also remind white labor leaders that they still need to address racism.

In addition to "talking truth to power," Joe walks the walk. During the 1980s, he organized the "Overground Railroad" voter registration drives. The civil rights movement used a majority of its resources to register Black Southern voters, but by the 1980s, the percentage of Northern Black voters was low.

Joe's show is not just an avenue to burn off steam — it serves as a vehicle for social change. As a child of the civil rights generation, Joe was exposed to civil rights activism. He witnessed the courage of the Little Rock Nine in 1957 on television, as well as the work of the Student Nonviolent Coordinating Committee and the Black Panthers. What they all had in common was they were young, idealistic, organized and intelligent young Black folks who wanted to improve the nation.

If you are a frequent listener to the Black Eagle Show on SiriusXM, you will hear all of the issues that impact Black folk, including police brutality, economic inequality and educational issues. Some of his weekly guests are financial experts who provide vital information for his audience. Joe has intelligent callers from a variety of backgrounds — truckers, lawyers, small business owners and teachers — and most can analyze and articulate the problem. Joe always says if an issue impacts a certain segment of the Black community, one of his listeners will call to share their perspective. Or as he says, "You never know who is listening to the Joe Madison show."

Whenever a first-time caller calls in to his show, Joe plays "Hallelujah." After the caller gives an intelligent two-minute rant, he simply asks the caller, "What are you going to do about it?" After Joe asks that simple question, there is a moment of silence because the caller usually did not anticipate Joe's response. They thought Joe would just agree with their comments, bitch and moan and not ask the caller to do anything to change the situation.

On the other hand, there are numerous callers who take on Joe's challenge and act. They may call a program manager at a conservative station to protest a racist remark, or they may take their money out of white-owned banks that take advantage of African American borrowers, or they may call out companies with CEOs making huge profits while laying people off.

Joe always says "you need to listen with a third ear" — hearing not just what is said, but the meaning that lies in between the words. Well, hopefully his story will force you to "read with a third eye" and inspire us to get up and do something.

Dave Canton, Ph.D.
Director of African American Studies Program
University of Florida, Gainesville

PREFACE

THE GUY ON THE RADIO

They call me the "Black Eagle." But I bet you don't know why.

I came up with the name "Black Eagle" in the early '90s during a meeting at WRC radio in Washington, D.C.

The station executives had hired a consultant to suggest ways to improve our station's programming. All the radio personalities were in the room, including Oliver North, the infamous lieutenant colonel from the Iran-Contra affair. As soon as the consultant saw North, he started praising him as the star of the station. The consultant told North that he was very popular and the people liked talking to him.

"You are the Captain Kirk of the Starship Enterprise," the consultant said to North, while the other hosts sat silently, annoyed.

So I spoke up. "Well, what about the rest of us? You know, we're not oatmeal. What about us?"

"Yeah, yeah, yeah," the consultant said. He was star-struck by Oliver North. The rest of us didn't matter.

After that meeting, I realized that I needed a handle, a radio name. The consultant had given Oliver a handle, Captain Kirk. So I said to myself, "You know what, why don't I call myself the Black Eagle?" My thinking was the eagle is our national bird and I am Black. Moreover, I thought the Black Eagle was original because I had never heard of a black eagle. I did not know if people would call in and say, "Well, there's no such thing as a black eagle so why are you using that name?"

One day I picked up my old friend, comedian and activist Dick

Gregory, and as I often do, I bounced some ideas off of him. "Have you ever heard of a black eagle?" I asked him. Dick cracked up. "Well, no, I've never heard of a black eagle, but I've got a feeling we are going to hear about it on the radio pretty soon." I told him I was considering calling myself the Black Eagle. Dick said, "Go for it," and so I started using it.

But not everyone had the same reaction. My white listeners called in and told me, "It's racist that you would call yourself a black eagle." One caller who I would never forget called in and said, "Well, if you gonna be the Black Eagle, I'm gonna be the White Dove." My response: "That's OK. Eagles eat doves."

So I kept using the name the Black Eagle. A few weeks later, the National Geographic channel was airing a show on eagles and, behold, they start talking about a black eagle, saying it was one of the largest species of eagles — the torso alone of an adult black eagle can measure over two feet long. A bird of prey, the black eagle is found in Tanzania and it has a seven-foot wingspan.

My wife, Sherry, worked at United Airlines in Bethesda, Maryland. I was in her office and the owner of a local art gallery walked in one day and saw my name and said, "Joe Madison!" I said, "Yeah."

"Are you the guy that talks on the radio?" I said yes. He had heard me refer to myself as the Black Eagle and asked, "Have you ever seen one?" I said no.

He owned an art gallery and he told me that he knows an artist who does wildlife, particularly birds. He told me that the artist had painted a portrait of a black eagle. He said I should go to his studio and take a look at the black eagle portrait. I saw the picture — a beautiful black eagle sitting on huge rocks overlooking the Serengeti — and fell in love with it. I bought it and it hangs in my home studio to this day.

Another time, I met a man — I think his name was Babb — who was an older guy who grew up in Harlem and was the leader of a band. He came to a live remote and told me he had a book titled *The Black Eagle* by John Peer Nugent. It was a biography of Col. Hubert Fauntleroy Julian, who was known as the "the Black Eagle of Harlem." He gave me a copy of the book and said, "I knew Mr. Julian when I was a little kid growing up in Harlem." He said Julian used to come into his father's store and he was quite a character. He was a famous Black pilot and contemporary of Charles Lindbergh. In 1922 he entered the Long Island Air Show, and became the first African American to parachute from a plane over New

York City. Two years later he announced his intention to fly from New York to Africa but did not get any farther than Flushing Bay, into which his plane crashed, but the attempt made him world-famous and resulted in his being dubbed "the Black Eagle."

The journalist H. Allen Smith reported that Julian had floated from the sky like a "black eagle," and that's how he got his name.

Julian was something else. He had a number of interesting jobs. He was a pilot for religious leader Father Divine. He was a gunrunner who sold arms in Africa and in Cuba. The State Department provided clearances for Julian when it was unheard of for Black folks. Julian even served as a pilot for Haile Selassie, the emperor of Ethiopia. Selassie assigned Julian to train pilots for Ethiopia's Imperial Air Force — which had only two Junkers monoplanes and a de Havilland DH.60 "Gipsy Moth."

Using the handle "the Black Eagle" educated my listeners about the bird and about Julian. The nickname came to life at the United Nations. Our station and a number of talk radio stations had a live remote at the United Nations. A woman, the No. 2 person from Tanzania at the United Nations, walked up to radio row and said, "Where is the Black Eagle?" Someone pointed to me. The woman walked over with her entourage and sat down for an interview. She promptly said, "This is the only interview I'm doing because you honor us and my country by referring to yourself as the Black Eagle because that is our national bird." After our interview she got up, walked out and did not give anybody else an interview.

One year I gave a speech on the Dr. Martin Luther King Jr. holiday at Joint Base Myer-Henderson Hall at Arlington National Cemetery in Virginia. The base commander said he had listened to my show. "I hear you often refer to yourself as the Black Eagle, and I have one upstairs."

"I am presenting you with a badge, a colonel's badge," he added. It was a black eagle. The commander told me that I am officially a black eagle. He said the next time I run into Oliver North, I should let him know that I am a full colonel and not a lieutenant colonel.

And now I can show him my black eagle emblem to prove it.

CHAPTER 1

INTO THE WAR ZONE

I flew into the war zone in South Sudan in a tiny, dilapidated old Russian plane where we were sitting on benches along the sides, leaning on barrels full of airplane fuel.

My wife, Sherry, a former flight attendant, noticed that the seatbelts didn't work — either one side of the buckle was missing or the other. So she tried tying the two parts of the canvas seatbelt into a knot across her waist.

I laughed and said, "Why bother? If the crash doesn't kill us, the fuel certainly will."

I had flown into South Sudan several times before, on a mission of mercy to deliver desperately needed supplies to war-torn villages — and to deliver cash money to buy the freedom of enslaved women and children kidnapped by brutal Arab militias.

Usually these rickety little planes had to fly a zigzag pattern to avoid ground fire, but South Sudan was currently experiencing a rare outbreak of peace because of a recently negotiated truce in a 22-year-old civil war. So there was little danger now of being shot out of the air, though the old propeller plane we had chartered out of Nairobi posed plenty of dangers of its own.

We flew into a tiny village in the bush where the "airport" was a crude little dirt strip the locals had cleared. The plane had to fly around the village a few times to alert the townspeople to shoo the goats and cows off the landing strip.

Usually when you fly, you have to put your tray table in the upright and locked position before landing. In this case, the only thing in the upright and locked position was our hands, praying for a safe landing.

We landed safely. Welcome to South Sudan! There to greet us were the leaders and the curious locals in threadbare clothes, scarred by two decades of war and atrocities, who all lived in mud huts and went to the bathroom in a hole in the ground.

We brought what we called "sacks of hope" — mosquito nets, cooking pots, farming tools, seeds, fishing hooks and tarps to replace their burned-out huts, which had been destroyed by slave raiders.

South Sudan is largely Black and Christian or animist, while northern Sudan is largely Arab and Islamic. One of the world's longest civil wars raged between these two combatants between 1983 and 2005, driven by religion, regionalism, competition for scarce resources and sheer brutality.

The Janjaweed were especially bloodthirsty Arab militias that the official government in Khartoum used as surrogates to carry out its dirty work. These raiders would invade an unsuspecting village like this one, kill all the men, kidnap all the women and children, and burn all the huts. The women and children became slaves, used for sex and labor, and sold for cash to any buyer who had enough money.

We checked into our hotel — a tent that we brought with us. We were running low on water, so I went to the local well, where women were waiting in line to use the malfunctioning old pump to bring up some really questionable water, a few squirts at a time.

One woman was pumping, pumping, pumping, working really hard to get the pump to work. So I offered to help, and I pumped vigorously until I was able to offer her just one tin cup full of water.

The entire line of women broke into uproarious laughter. Mystified, I looked to our translator, who explained that according to the customs of these people, I had just asked this woman to marry me.

"So Joe just proposed to her," says Sherry. "I went up and took him by the hand and pulled him away. And they laughed even more, because women didn't just go up and touch their man like that. I said, 'No, he's already taken.'"

Our primary mission in South Sudan was to liberate women and children who had been captured as slaves, and we did this by posing as slave buyers. We had money raised by Christianity Solidarity

International, a humanitarian organization in Zurich, Switzerland, and I raised some of the money on my radio show as well.

So Christian Solidarity International would send Sudanese men to go north and buy the freedom of these women and children. And they would meet them in some isolated area in the bush, pretending to be slavers, and would turn over wheelbarrows full of Sudanese currency, paying cash for these people. A woman was worth about $35, whereas a goat was worth about $50. The northern Sudanese did not realize that these people were going to be freed.

But one night we were out in a convoy of jeeps delivering these "sacks of hope." It was very late at night, pitch-black — you couldn't see your hand in front of your face. Sherry was in one vehicle, I was in another. And the "road" was just a crude dirt track in the bush.

All of a sudden, our caravan had to stop at this makeshift checkpoint, which was basically a tree across the road and some folding chairs. There were three or four young South Sudanese soldiers in ragtag uniforms, with automatic rifles, and they ordered us out of the vehicles. It was totally dark — no light except our headlights.

And I thought: This is it. This is the end. We didn't know who they were, I didn't know where we were, I didn't know what was being said. There's no way I would be able to protect Sherry, who was one or two vehicles behind me. I thought, we could be killed and dragged into the bush and potentially never found.

"I was thinking the same thing," says Sherry. "I thought, here we are, separated, and we may very likely die here tonight on this dark, dusty road. And who would notify our families, who would tell our children? What on earth have we gotten ourselves into?"

Riding in the car with me was a man named Angelo Marac, who had been a commander in the South Sudanese army, and was now a politician, a lawmaker in the national legislature. I had known him for a while, and he had always been a soft-spoken, gentle man with an easy smile. He told us not to get out of the vehicle.

But he did get out, and the instant he did, his demeanor changed. He suddenly adopted this posture of authority and fury, and he started shouting at these rogue soldiers. I don't speak Dinka, and I don't know what he was saying, but it sounded something like, "Who the hell are you, and what the fuck do you think you're doing?"

And these soldiers recognized him as their former commander!

They immediately apologized. And next thing you know, the roadblock was removed and we were on our way.

Just another day in the life of a guy who's supposed to be making a living talking on the radio....

CHAPTER 2

GENESIS OF AN ACTIVIST

....

This is the first time I have ever told this story publicly.

I was born on June 16, 1949, in Dayton, Ohio. My mother was named Nancy Stone, and the man I knew as my father was named Felix Madison. As we'll see, I learned very late in life that Felix Madison was not really my biological father, but I certainly didn't know that as a child, and I don't think he did either.

What I do know is that my parents abandoned my sister and me when I was about 2 years old. The only explanation I ever got was from my grandmother, Betty Lou Stone, who told me when I was an adolescent how my grandfather found my sister and me alone in our house one day. My grandmother said I was about 2 years old, my sister was a year younger, and I was trying to change her diaper. My grandfather brought us to his home, and our grandparents raised us from that day forward.

Not knowing how my parents met or the circumstances of how my sister and I came to be abandoned has always remained an enigma to me. Adults in those days didn't talk about those things, especially around children.

My grandfather was a very influential figure in my life. His name was Big Jim Stone, and he was a 6-foot-8 prizefighter during the Jack Johnson era. Jack Johnson was the first African American heavyweight champion, in the days when boxers fought bare-fisted.

Jim Stone was born in Clarksdale, Mississippi, and he had a sixth-grade education. He had to leave home after he got into a fight with a white man — and almost killed him. Before the white folks could get revenge, he moved to Memphis, Tennessee, and later to Rochester, New York. This is where he first became a prizefighter. He was often in the press and began to fight worldwide, although most of his fights were in Canada. He was pretty successful and made a fair amount of money, but he soon gambled it all away.

My grandfather eventually got married (twice), moved to Dayton, Ohio, and had two children — my mother and a son who died from a burst appendix at age 5. He told me that the death could have been prevented, but back then, Blacks received poor medical care in Dayton. The doctor had actually misdiagnosed the condition altogether. Every Memorial Day, my family and I still place flowers on my uncle's gravesite and whenever I'm in Dayton I always visit.

My grandfather also worked as a garbage man. He'd wake up at 4 in the morning and did not return home until early evening. He got paid to haul trash from businesses and apartments to a landfill in his raggedy trash truck. When times were tough, he'd also haul household garbage. During the summer when I was out of school, I worked with him. I'd help him haul trash, but I also looked through the dump and pulled out metals — aluminum, tin and copper — and collected rags, cardboard and newspapers. I organized them into piles. On Saturdays, I loaded everything onto a truck, and we drove to the junkyard (today they call them "recycling centers"). My pay was based on the going price of paper, cardboard and metal. So we had two flows of income from that business.

Most Black people in Dayton were working hard jobs and constantly looking for work, so this was nothing out of the ordinary. I did this for a dozen years.

My grandfather's first wife (my mother's mother) was named Ethel Waters — like the famous jazz singer. She was from Bangor, Maine, and may have met my grandfather while he was prizefighting in Canada. I believe they divorced after their son died. My grandfather later married the woman I knew as my grandmother, Betty Lou Johnson from Tennessee. She was lighter than Lena Horne, had straight hair, and could have passed for white. After she passed away, I got a copy of her birth certificate and noticed that the racial categories Black and white were not checked. Instead, the white doctor wrote in "darkie."

He wanted to make sure that nobody had the audacity to think she was white.

Betty Lou had an eighth-grade education and worked as a housekeeper in white suburban communities. She'd leave the house early in the morning, so my sister and I got ourselves up, dressed, made breakfast and got ourselves to school. We'd spend part of the summer visiting extended family in Clarksdale. My grandparents dropped my sister and me off at my cousin's house and came back later in the summer to pick us up. Clarksdale was a small, rural Black town with cotton fields. All of my cousins laughed at me because I didn't know anything about the country. When we swam in the creeks, they'd scare us by saying that water moccasins would bite us.

When we drove through Mississippi and approached a small town, we'd slow down. My grandmother always told my grandfather, "Jim, slow down. You don't want to get a ticket and risk getting thrown in jail down here. You know these crackers will throw you in jail."

One time, we were visiting my great-grandmother in Cincinnati and stopped on the side of the road to relieve ourselves. Even in southern Ohio, Blacks could not stop at white-owned gas stations to use the restrooms. Think of the indignity of your grandmother having to lift up her skirt on the side of the road while cars were passing by. We'd ask, "Why don't you stop at the gas station up there?" They'd just say, "Nah, that's OK. We'll take care of it out here." My grandmother even brought fried chicken, coleslaw and potato salad on our road trips because Black folk could not stop and eat at white restaurants.

The man I knew as my father, Felix Madison, was born in Montrose, Mississippi, and served in the Navy during World War II. After the Navy, he met and married my mother. They then divorced and went their separate ways. Eventually my dad moved to Flint, Michigan, and worked at the Buick factory. He was real cool and dressed well. Once, when I was visiting him, he took one look at me and said, "Go upstairs and put on some clothes." I don't remember what I had on, but whenever I went out with him, he insisted that I look clean.

My mother, Nan, was born in Dayton. After she abandoned us, she was in and out of my life. She moved to Indianapolis and remarried twice. She would visit Dayton sometimes, and during the summer, my sister and I lived with her in Indianapolis. Eventually she settled in Dayton, where she worked as a census enumerator — someone who goes door-to-door to count people for the U.S. Census Bureau every 10 years — and she also became a community activist. She worked on voter registration drives and assisted Black people in the community.

My sister, Yvonne, had a difficult life in Dayton. She tried hard but didn't do well in school. She worked primarily minimum wage jobs or received welfare and also became a single mother — eventually ending up having four children. She married but later divorced. Once I went to college, I could only visit her during breaks, so it was very difficult to maintain a close relationship.

BLOCKBUSTING

My family was working class. Sometimes you hear poor people say, "We don't consider ourselves poor." However, in our case, we knew we were poor. We had less than the doctor, the mortician and even the teacher living in our neighborhood. But although we did not have what other kids had, my grandparents forbade us from using that as an excuse not to succeed.

Dayton, like most Northern cities, was essentially a segregated city. While segregation is a legal term, people need to understand that de facto segregation still existed in the North. Black folks lived on the west side of Dayton with only small pockets of middle-class whites. At Jackson Elementary School, Black and white children would walk home from school together and play with each other on the playground. But by the early sixties, most of the white families had started to leave. Starting in elementary school, my class pictures contained fewer and fewer white kids. In kindergarten, there were 10 white students; in junior high, there were four; and by high school, there was one. Nobody was overtly racist, but by the time I got to high school, racism had become more evident.

With desegregation, housing barriers were broken. Clarence Bowman, a Black mortician, moved into an all-white neighborhood. He purchased a one-level ranch house, which we all thought was a mansion. The local newspaper quoted him as saying to Black people, "Do not move on my block." His controversial statements caused an uproar in the Black community. My grandparents and other Black folk debated his statement. Many said, "What's with this uppity Negro telling folks not to move next door to him?"

When I was older, I realized what he meant.

Mr. Bowman wanted African Americans to move to the *next* block in the white neighborhood because if too many Black people moved into the same area, white real estate agents would say, "Black people are moving into your neighborhood. You need to sell now because the value of your home is going to decrease." His comments were a warning to Blacks. He was essentially saying, "Don't let them block-bust. Skip around. Go over there. Don't all come over here."

Much later, when I moved to Detroit in the mid-seventies, I bought my first house in a neighborhood that was becoming Black. I had a Black neighbor on one side and a white neighbor on the other. One day, a real estate agent called me up and said, "You know, some Black folk are moving into the neighborhood and maybe you ought to think about selling." I played along and said, "Really? Do you know who these folks are? And how much do you think we can get for our house now?" I was just joking and did not sell, but I remembered what Clarence Bowman had said.

Many in the Black community did not talk about blockbusting. But in Dayton, it was real.

THE DOWNTOWN 'Y'

There were two YMCAs in Dayton. The 5th Street YMCA was for Black folk and the downtown YMCA was for whites. One day, Mr. Leo Lucas, the only Black on the school board, paid for me to join the downtown YMCA. I was actually one of only three Black kids who had ever jumped into this particular swimming pool — and in those days, we swam naked. I remember thinking, "Oh, this is a really big-ass pool." When I got older, I was invited to give a talk in Dayton and Mr. Lucas was in the audience. I told the story of how he paid for my YMCA membership. After the event, I spoke to Mr. Lucas, whose health was failing. He said, "You know why I did that, don't you?" I said, "I never knew why." He said, "Because we had to integrate the downtown YMCA and wanted to send the best." I had no idea. I just thought I was the luckiest kid in the world because I got to take a bus downtown and go to the YMCA. I had no idea that folks were testing to see if the white YMCA would allow us to use the pool (and were picking boys who wouldn't steal the white folks' stuff). This was a civil rights moment in Dayton that I (unknowingly) played a part in.

I attended Roosevelt High School, which was named after President Theodore Roosevelt. Our school's mascot was a teddy bear. I was told that when the school was predominantly white, it was a white bear. When it became predominantly Black, it became a black bear. That may have been an urban legend, but many teachers told us that. Roosevelt High School was actually the only school in Dayton with two swimming pools — a small one for Black kids and a large one for white kids. Roosevelt High also had two gyms. Black students used the smaller gym, white students used the larger gym.

In 1960, Roosevelt High School was a predominantly white school. But when I arrived in 1964, it was 99 percent Black. The majority of the remaining teachers were, frankly, old as hell. They had taught so many years that they couldn't transfer to other schools. I believe the majority felt trapped. Fortunately, there were some good ones who were not hostile to Black students and would even go the extra mile for us. But by the mid-sixties, they were encountering a whole new culture of students. Also, the majority of younger teachers believed the school board had intentionally assigned them to a less desirable school. While most Black teachers had high expectations, the majority of white teachers had low expectations. As a result, white teachers tended to track Black students into easier courses.

My grandparents often told me, "You gotta be twice as good at what you do to get ahead in this society." So while I was an athlete and played ball with folks from different backgrounds and academic skills, I always wanted to hang out with the smart kids. I never allowed myself to be undervalued or marginalized. However, there were times when teachers attempted to do this. When there was an award or a competition, certain teachers always selected white students. One teacher had to recommend students as candidates for student council and I was not selected, although my peers recognized me as a student leader. I was captain of the football team and president of the Varsity Club (the largest club at Roosevelt). Every student athlete who had received a varsity letter was part of the club. Still, I was not recommended for student council. I asked the teacher, Miss Loretta B. Dwyer, "Why didn't you select me?"

"You know, Joe Madison, if you ever decided to take yourself seriously, there's no telling what you could be," she said. "And maybe this just might be a kick in the pants for you to realize your potential. So, no, I am not recommending you for the student council this time around but maybe next semester."

I never forgot Miss Dwyer's statement — or her refusal to accept any written paper unless it had a yellow ribbon in the upper left-hand corner of the paper. I had no idea why. She wouldn't have given a damn if Alexander Pope or Paul Laurence Dunbar had written the paper. It had to have a yellow ribbon. Imagine a bunch of inner-city dudes running around trying to get yellow ribbons to put on their papers. She never told us why she wanted that yellow ribbon. She resigned just a couple of years after I graduated. On her last day, she was sitting at her desk in the classroom and students threw eggs at her. She may have been 90 years old, and it was really sad.

"Mr. Mouse" was my white chemistry teacher. I remember him because he looked like a mouse — he had a little pointed nose and pointy ears. I did not learn a lick of chemistry from him. On the first day of class, he announced to his all-Black classroom that he had just returned from Vietnam and added, "I really didn't want to teach here." He told us that he asked to teach at Meadowdale, a predominantly white school across town but the school board assigned him to my school because he was a new teacher.

Mr. Mouse was a helicopter pilot in Vietnam and had filmed some of his missions. As a result, we spent the majority of the school year watching his combat films from the war. He showed us film of himself blowing up and shooting people. I think he suffered from what today they call "post-traumatic stress disorder," but we didn't know anything about it back in those days. We also didn't know what the Vietnam War was really about. All we knew was that in 1966, Muhammad Ali — who had changed his name from Cassius Clay two years earlier — had refused to be drafted for the war. I knew some folks who were being drafted. However, I was a junior in high school and too young for the draft.

I never will forget the content of the films. After I watched them, I asked, "What in the hell is Vietnam? What is going on in Vietnam?"

One of the black-and-white films showed Vietnamese walking across rice paddies. "Now watch this!" Mr. Mouse yelled from the back of the room. A rocket then shot from his helicopter and blew a man up. We sat there horrified with our mouths wide open. Remember, this was my *chemistry* class. Mr. Mouse made it through the school year, but two years later, he was gone. When I later took college chemistry, it was like starting all over again.

My English teacher, Sarah Roweton, was a nice lady with a love of the subject. I remember one time she asked us, "Y'all don't have the complete works of Shakespeare in your home?" She had no idea that we were lucky if we had a complete set of encyclopedias at home — a full set cost about $350 back then, or about $2,700 in today's dollars. She talked a lot about the importance of reading English literature, but I didn't really appreciate it until I was older.

Ms. Dorothy Bush, my human relations teacher — today, we'd call that sociology — required that we read the newspapers and know what was going on in the news. Every day, she'd have us debate local and national issues as she guided us and helped us enhance our skills. She thought that I was a really good public speaker. So that year, when a social club called the Roundtable was sponsoring its annual citywide oratorical contest, our school liaison, Mr. Robert Amos, a white history teacher, invited me to compete. I agreed and wrote a speech about the civil rights movement and how the nation must continue to support the movement. I practiced on weekends and in the evenings, and every Saturday, I'd work with Mr. Amos in his yard. We pulled weeds, planted flowers and practiced my speech. In between, he spent time correcting my diction.

Our high school allowed a number of students to speak during commencement and the faculty handed out Theodore Roosevelt statues for the No. 1 student in the graduating class and for each specific class like calculus, chemistry and algebra. I was an average student on the college preparatory track and had struggled with Latin. However, I finished in the top 25 percent of my class, had good enough grades to be one of the commencement speakers and received an award in human relations, which was a class that examined social issues.

BUSTED OVER A BUTTON

Soon, it was time for the first round of the oratorical contest, which was held in Dayton. I was the only Black male student and I won. I don't know how many students competed in Dayton, but it didn't matter. I was moving forward to regionals. The winner of the regional contest would receive a scholarship and win a paid trip out West to attend the Roundtable national convention. I wanted to be that guy.

Now, I didn't know that the Roundtable — an all-white club — was like the Optimist Club or the Lion's Club. However, when I got to the regional competition there were only two competitors left — a white student and me. I gave my speech and the judges announced the winner. I had lost by three points. I asked my teacher, "Why did I lose by three points? Was it style?"

"No."

"Delivery?"

"No."

"Content?"

"No."

They said I had simply forgotten to button the middle button on my suit jacket.

Mr. Amos was mild-mannered but when he heard about that, he went bonkers. He believed that the white judges were simply refusing to send a Black kid from Dayton to represent this organization.

My most memorable moments in high school were on the football field. Roosevelt had great athletes and many attended Division I college athletic programs. During my senior year, we had the No. 1 football player in the state, Leo Hayden, and the No. 1 basketball player in the state, Rudy Benjamin.

In 1966, our football team was the third-ranked team in the nation. During that season, we beat a team from Dayton 90-0 and made it to the city championship. We then played Belmont — an all-white, working-class, blue-collar team — located on the other side of town.

Big Jim Caldwell was the Black coach with Belmont. He had graduated from Dunbar High School in Dayton, and he was known as "the Enforcer." He weighed 360 pounds and had played professional football for the Chicago Bears. Richard Marquardt was our white head coach. To this day, we blame him for our disappointing loss that day. Marquardt relied too much on our fullback, Leo Hayden. If we ran 20 plays, Leo got the ball 19 times. It didn't take a defensive genius to figure out our offense.

My teammates and I asked, "Why in the hell does he keep running this dude?"

I looked at the game with Belmont as just another football game because I had not understood the racial aspect of it. However, we lost that day and felt that we let down the entire west side of Dayton. I did not understand this until I spoke with my future father-in-law, Don

Crawford, the first Black city councilman — he had actually bet some money on that game. Prior to the game, he was bragging to his white colleagues on the city council that Roosevelt would win.

The local newspapers did not discuss the racial aspect of the game because it was unspoken. But as I got older, I realized its significance.

Paul Laurence Dunbar High School was on the west side of Dayton, and it was a predominantly Black school. My mother had actually graduated from Dunbar. The students there studied Langston Hughes and the Harlem Renaissance because their teachers were Black. They were also assigned plays based on the works of Black artists such as Lorraine Hansberry's "Raisin in the Sun." At my school, we did a play called "Arsenic and Old Lace," written by Joseph Kesselring, and I played Jonathan Brewster, the crazy uncle who thought he was Teddy Roosevelt. Before then I had never heard of "Arsenic and Old Lace."

The white teachers were teaching us their culture — Walt Whitman, Ernest Hemingway, William Faulkner.

There was a young brother who, to this day, is my best friend, Dr. Arthur Thomas. Dr. Thomas was a militant Negro and the principal of Garfield Elementary School. He ran a summer program that enabled me to work in the library and not at the dump with my granddad. He served as an advisor. On some days before work, he brought a group of us together and taught us African American history. He told us, "Many of you, because of the civil rights movement, are now going to be first-generation athletes. You're going to run into racism, so you have to know who you are." So, he taught us how to deal with it.

Dr. Thomas grew up in Philadelphia and was best friends with Bill Cosby. In high school, his white teachers told him he wouldn't amount to anything. However, after he graduated from college, he returned to his high school and said, "Here's my degree. You said I'd never amount to anything." After he received his master's degree, he returned again and said, "By the way, here's my master's degree." And then he walked out the door. After he received his doctorate degree instead of going to the school he said, "I decided to mail a copy of it."

Dr. Thomas served as the president of Central State University (a Black university in Wilberforce, Ohio), created relationships between Central State University and Africa, started student exchange programs and improved the School of Communications. He was an activist and prepared me for racism in college, even though I had already encountered plenty of racism in high school.

THE 'BLUE VEIN' CHURCH

I attended Mt. Calvary Baptist Church, which was a traditional Black Baptist church. The sermons at Mt. Calvary focused on staying out of hell, and there was a great deal of "hootin' and hollerin'." I never got anything out of that, but I joined a youth choir called the Sunshine Band. They only knew two songs: "This Little Light of Mine" and "Jesus Loves Me." However, the choir exposed me to music. I ended up singing in my junior high, high school and college choirs.

When I was attending Mt. Calvary, I had a newspaper delivery job. And like most of the paperboys, I was a Cub Scout. We held our meetings at St. Margaret's Episcopal church. When I first told my family that we had our meetings at an Episcopalian church, all hell broke loose because my mother, grandfather and grandmother were all Baptists. At the time, I could barely spell Episcopalian.

On one Sunday morning, I was sitting in church between my grandmother and another woman. The other woman caught the Holy Ghost and slapped me in the head with her pocketbook. It was not intentional, but "the spirit" had gotten into her. I said, "To hell with this." And then I got up, left, walked down the street and joined the Episcopalians.

Now, my grandparents were not happy with my decision to join St. Margaret's. In fact, they had referred to it as a "blue vein church." That meant that the church only accepted light-skinned African Americans. This always struck me as interesting because my grandmother was as white as a saucer.

In spite of my family's reservations, I was an acolyte because I wanted to become a priest. I was president of the Young Churchmen, and St. Margaret's quickly became my church home. I really loved that church. The first person I met there was Billy Marable. He was later known as Dr. Manning Marable and became a professor of history and African American studies at Columbia University. He was also the author of the award-winning biography *Malcolm X — A Life of Reinvention*.

Billy was a pernicious kid. I'm surprised that he turned out to be such a successful public intellectual and scholar because he was very quiet and unassuming. I think his father was a teacher and businessman.

He owned a photography shop and took prom and wedding photos. The Marables were all members of the church. The majority of its members were college-educated professionals — doctors, lawyers and teachers.

I liked the service at St. Margaret's because, frankly, it was shorter than the Baptist service. More importantly, Father M.B. Cochran was a forward-thinking priest who embraced liberation theology. Once I convinced him to hold a New Year's Eve dance for kids on the lower level of the church. We could never do that at Mt. Calvary church. He said, "Sure, however, all of your friends have to turn off the music at 11 and come upstairs and attend midnight mass to pray and count down to the new year. At the end of the service, you can go back downstairs and continue with your party." Parents also supported that dance because it was a safe place to send their children. Some people who didn't even attend the service that night dropped off their kids at the church.

In high school, everybody wanted to be part of a singing group. This was the era of Motown and Stax Records. One could find men in Dayton singing under streetlights — like you'd see in Detroit and New York. We all wanted to be the future Four Tops or Temptations, and a number of us formed funk groups. Many of us also sang in the choir and played in the band. We'd perform at local skating rink parties and dances.

Our parents and teachers never really insisted that we get involved in the civil rights movement. But they never hid it from us. My first hero in the civil rights movement was Ernie Green from the Little Rock Nine. I remember watching the Little Rock Nine on television. I was in middle school and remember seeing Black teenagers and thinking to myself how much courage they had. I marveled at the abuse they endured just to get an education. After watching them on television, my attitude was that if they were willing to be spat upon by white students, education must be very important. I saw the Little Rock Nine as my big brothers and sisters.

FROM 'THE OTHER SIDE OF THE TRACKS'

I had a number of girlfriends in high school. One was Father Cochran's daughter and another was the Black councilman's daughter, Donnella Crawford. Her father was the first Black city councilman in Dayton, Ohio, and he was really a cool dude. He was suave, political, smart, well-spoken, well-dressed, and he knew city government. Donnella and I eventually married in 1974, even though I was the guy from the other side of town. She majored in journalism and advertising at Northwestern University. Your father could be a doctor, college president or professor, but to whites, you were still a nigger who lived on the west side of town. I also happened to live on "the other side of the tracks" since the railroad ran straight down the middle of our Black community.

So Donnella and I had a long-distance romance going on because I was up in Wisconsin at a small college for a couple of years, while she was down near Chicago. But she was a brilliant woman. She always wanted to be a journalist, so of course she went to the Medill School of Journalism at Northwestern University in Evanston. She went on to work in television and became an award-winning producer.

We had a daughter named Shawna while we were in Detroit, Michigan, and Shawna grew up in radio. She later became the call screener for my show at SiriusXM. Shawna was probably 12 years old and screening phone calls for me on the radio. Now, Shawna has her own TV and radio show for Voice of America. She graduated from Howard University School of Communications. Upon graduation, she went to work for me as my producer when I was at WRC in Washington, D.C. And then, poor thing, the station got sold, so we both got fired. She then went to Baltimore as my producer at WOLB. Later, she got her own show as a morning personality at the Radio One station, WERQ-92Q. Then she went to work for Worldspace, which was a forerunner to XM radio, and it was a global satellite entity. At the same time, she was at WPGC, fill-in hosting a show called "Love Talk and Slow Jams." When XM branched out, she worked as a program director for Worldspace, where she programmed an international channel called World for XM. After that, she was my producer at SiriusXM. I also had my own show on SiriusXM called "Cocoa Mode," talking about pop culture, since everybody else was doing the political thing. Finally, after a couple of years, she got hired at Voice of America, where she is a program director and has her own radio show that's heard globally. Shawna is an outstanding broadcaster.

Donnella and I divorced in 1977 and I met Sharon Moore, my second and current wife, who was living in Detroit at the time. Sherry, as I call her, had a 30-year career with United Airlines. She worked as an executive assistant to the vice president of United Airlines when I first met her and managed the airline's operations at the Detroit airport for United. She retired after 35 years. After retirement I asked her to come and be my executive producer when I went over to Sirius. So, the agreement was that Sirius hired both Sherry and me. She has been my executive producer ever since I've been there.

'YOU GOT TO REALLY KNOW WHO YOU ARE'

In Dayton, the majority of police officers were white and widely seen as racist. They would constantly stop and harass Black drivers. The Miami River runs through Dayton and there is a bridge. One night, we were marching down the bridge heading downtown. Folks were throwing rocks and breaking out windows on Third Street. This was nothing major like the Philadelphia riot in 1964 or the Detroit riot in 1967. However, the police stopped us at the bridge and did not allow us to go downtown. There were a few squad cars lined up, and they said, "You should turn around and go back to where you came from." This was my first experience with civil disobedience.

I ended up attending Wisconsin State University at Whitewater, a predominantly white university. I was actually the first Black person that many white students had ever met. So I wasn't surprised that I stumbled across a number of cultural differences. For example, it was the first time I'd discovered that macaroni and cheese could be served as an entrée. Where I grew up, mac and cheese was a side dish. When I went to the cafeteria, I asked the cafeteria worker, "Where's the beef?" She responded, "Well, today we have macaroni and cheese." I said, "I understand that, but where's the beef?" She again said, "That's the entrée." I said, "Who in the hell ever ate macaroni and cheese by itself?"

Wisconsin State, Whitewater had a great Division III football program. Still, we had a number of those smart-ass, talking-shit, white boy suburbanites on our team. When I'd go to practice, I'd beat up on those folks, especially when I became middle linebacker. My high school coach Richard Marquardt taught me well. Since he had played in the pros, he taught me how to tackle and shed blockers. One day, when the whistle blew, I was whupping ass so bad that I cracked a white player's helmet and gave him a concussion. I overheard my coach say, "We'd better make this boy starting middle linebacker or he's gonna kill our running back." Keep in mind that in the 1960s, African Americans did not play quarterback, center or middle linebacker. Whites thought that Blacks were not smart enough to play those positions. That's why I kicked ass when I was out on the field.

Going to Wisconsin State University was a difficult experience for me. There were only three Black players on the football team, and they were quiet as church mice. I remember the isolation and marginalization, but I remembered what Dr. Thomas told me the summer before: "You got to really know who you are."

Part of overcoming racism, I came to understand, is knowing who you are and being comfortable with that. Still, I thought I had made a terrible mistake by going to Wisconsin. This was what my parents and grandparents told me: "You gotta overcome it. We fought for you to get in here. Nobody said it was gonna be easy. So we assume you can do it. And if you don't do it, you've let us down. If you screw up and don't get good grades, you've let us down. If you let them get to you, you've let us down. If you don't make the football team, you've let us down."

During the late '60s, many whites thought that all Black people were potential Black Panthers. I started college in 1966, two years before Dr. King was killed and the year the Black Panthers were founded in Oakland, California. Black college students always seemed to be asking, "Are you a Black Panther or are you nonviolent? Are you Malcolm or are you Martin?" The reality was Black students were a little bit of both, depending on how much whites pissed us off.

When I entered college, I just wanted to be a good Negro. I was a good kid, sang in the choir, played football and did everything white folks expected me to do. However, I still felt rejected. The majority of the white students, faculty and staff wondered if I really belonged there. These kinds of experiences made me question my existence sometimes. I would ask myself, "Why am I here? Wait a minute, these folks are making me question myself." I had to do the same thing to get into the same university as the white students, but I questioned my own existence. That's a hell of a thing. That's like someone walking into a restaurant and saying, "What are you two niggers doing sitting back here?" Well, wait a minute, I'm sitting here because I have a right to sit here like everybody else. I have a right to be on this campus like everybody else. The environment in Wisconsin was so hostile, though, they had me questioning myself.

During my freshman year, I was in the library one evening and picked up Lerone Bennett's *Before the Mayflower*. I stayed up all night and read the entire book. After I completed it, I broke down in tears. I was in the corner of the library basement and discovered how the past and present had all come together. I realized that white folks had no business marginalizing me. Although my first reaction was a flood of tears, my second reaction was anger. I was very angry because I realized that no one has the right to question the Black man's right to exist on this planet. I interpreted Bennett's book as saying that the United States was lucky that Black folk are here and we should be treated equally. Reading the book was my turning point and changed my attitude.

In 2007, I emceed a retirement party for Simeon Booker, the 90-year-old Washington editor at *Jet* magazine who first broke the Emmett Till story. Mr. Bennett was at the event. Meeting Bennett was like meeting Jesus Christ because his book had enlightened me and changed my life forever.

FIRST STEPS ON THE PATH

In 1967, the university invited Julian Bond, a former member of the Student Nonviolent Coordinating Committee (SNCC), to campus to give a talk. Bond had left Morehouse College in 1961 to become a full-time student activist. In 1965, he was elected to the Georgia House of Representatives, but in 1966 he was voted out of his position because of his anti-Vietnam War position. In 1967, the United States Supreme Court ruled 9-0 in the Bond v. Floyd case that the state had violated Bond's First Amendment rights. I volunteered and invited Bond to stay with me in my dorm room. We talked all night. By 1967, Bond was celebrating because of his civil rights activism and his recent return to office in Georgia. Bond invited me to travel with him for three days around Wisconsin. We remained friends until the day he died, and I have always considered Bond a mentor, even though he was only 27 years old when we met. When I returned to campus, I became the spokesman for the Black student movement on campus. This was what started my path into civil rights.

During the spring of my freshman year, Black students started making demands on campus. It started off as more symbolic. For instance, we wanted soul food in the cafeteria. However, there were no Black cooks who could cook black-eyed peas, so the cafeteria workers just opened a can and said, "Here's y'all's black-eyed peas." Also, there might have been 100 Black students on campus, but there were no Black professors. We demanded more African American courses in the curriculum, and we lobbied for Black History Week to be recognized.

After my freshman year, when I returned to Dayton in the summer, my former high school principal invited me to speak. In my speech, I cursed out the school's faculty. I said, "How dare you say that you educated us?" Of course, I was not talking about all of the teachers — I did have some good ones. However, I stated the issue frankly and asked the Black students, "OK, so what are you going do about it?" I told all of the students to get involved. Black students were the vanguards and guinea pigs of the civil rights movement. I said, "And by the way, we are not only taking a seat, but we are going to change the culture of this place." I said, "You are going to teach African American history and Africa is not a dark continent, damn it." I told the students that they should demand that administrators hire teachers who know how to teach Black history.

The summer before I was to return to the Wisconsin campus for my sophomore year, I faced a huge setback. I received a letter from the football coach saying, "We do not want you on the team anymore." I read that letter and was devastated. Football was a major part of my life and my "ticket out." I called the coach and said, "What is this?" He just said, "We just don't want your kind on the team."

I asked, "What does that mean?"

He again said, "We just don't want your kind on the team."

I asked, "Well, what does that fucking mean?"

He said, "You know what? You ought to be more like Charlie Robinson." Charlie was a teammate of mine — and still a close friend — who at the time was not nearly as active or militant as I was. Yet years later, Charlie was kicked off the team — and out of the school — for standing up for other Black students.

I was furious when the coach told me that. To this day, if I ever hear a white person say I should be like another Black person, I tell them that they can kiss my ass. The coach viewed Robinson as the right kind of Negro. He ended the call by saying, "That's my position and, you know, I'm the one who determines who plays." I really don't think it had anything to do with football or my grades. I suspect that he really didn't like me because I was involved in the social movement.

Looking back, that was the best thing that ever happened to me.

It's true — when one door closes, another one opens up. I returned to Dayton and spent a year working at the Inland steel factory. In August, I went to Atlanta to enroll at Morehouse College. However, when I arrived, they didn't have my transcripts. So when the football coach told me to come to practice, I had to tell him that the school didn't have my records. He said that it didn't matter, and that I could stay in the dormitory. To my surprise, it was an attic room with four guys and no desks. After I saw the room, I just said, "I'm leaving." I then got in my car and returned to Dayton.

I soon received a call from the coach at Washington University in St. Louis. The coach said, "I want you at Washington University, but there's a caveat. Your grades aren't quite good enough to transfer, so you have to go back to Wisconsin State, improve your grades, transfer and we'll redshirt you." Now, quite honestly, I had never heard of Washington University in St. Louis. I soon found out it was an academic powerhouse.

My hard work paid off. I earned an academic scholarship. Although I still could not afford Washington University, the coach told me they would take care of it. In addition to playing football, I sang in the Washington University choir, worked as a part-time statistician for the St. Louis Cardinals football team, and served as a DJ for KFRH, the campus radio station. I studied sociology with an emphasis in urban affairs, and I ended up earning my BA there in 1971.

When I transferred to Washington University for my junior and senior year, I continued singing in the concert choir. That is how I met Orland Johnson, our choir director. He was a very interesting white man from Texas who was a trained classical musician. But he loved jazz, so he hung out with Black jazz and blues artists while growing up in Texas. Since our choir traveled all over the country representing Washington University, Johnson made sure that I had a solo during our concert tours. He appreciated my pure bass voice. And the music we sang was — as my grandmother would say — very highbrow. But that's what I remember about him. I tried to track him down and finally went back to Washington University and met the current choir director, who said that he had passed away. I really miss him because he was just a down-to-earth kind of guy, you know, easy-going, but at the same time a disciplinarian.

I would go to choir early in the afternoon, and then I would leave rehearsal to attend football practice. You can imagine a lot of guys on my team thinking here is Madison coming out of choir rehearsals, where he sings classical music, to put on a football uniform and beat the hell out of people.

During my junior year, the choir took a trip to Washington, D.C., and we performed at the Watergate Terrace. The choir also traveled to New York City and we sang at Lincoln Center's Alice Tully Hall. These concerts occurred during the spring, but I still was made to work out in order to remain in shape.

ALWAYS MONEY IN MY POCKET

I didn't just sing and play football, I also had two jobs in college. One was as a statistician, which was a great opportunity because it provided me opportunities to hang out with pro players. This is how that job came about. During football season at Washington University, the public relations director for the St. Louis Cardinals football team (the baseball team was also called the Cardinals) traveled with our football team, and on one of the trips I was introduced to him. We struck up a conversation and I told him that I would like a job with the Cardinals. He said, "Well, you know, we've got an opening for a statistician on home games." And, man, that was one of the best jobs I ever had. I didn't make a lot of money, and I don't even remember what the salary was because it was just a stipend. But we got all the free beer we could drink and all the free sandwiches we could eat because we'd be in the press box. I also had the run of the clubhouse, so I got to know a lot of the ballplayers and hang out with them.

Cid Edwards was the fullback, and Jamie Rivers was a linebacker. Those two happened to also be from Ohio, so we hit it off. Ernie McMillan was a big tackle for them. I used to work out with the Cardinals, training with them in the clubhouse and working out with them during football season and offseason for those two years.

The other job I had was as a food runner in the morning at a hotel. I could not tell you the name of the hotel to this day, but the owner was a booster for the football team. I met him on the plane and said, "Do you got a job for me to make a little extra money?" And in those days you could make a little extra money doing almost anything. It was legal then. So, I made a little extra money by running food in the morning. I would wake up early in the morning, which was easy because I had always been getting up early to do morning paper routes. (Now that I think about it, mornings have been pretty good to me.) So, I would wake up early in the morning, go to this hotel where people would order their breakfast, then take the food to their hotel rooms. And every morning I'd walk away by 10 o'clock to my first college class with a pocket full of tip money. And the trick I learned was to never have change, especially early in the morning.

So, I'd go in and they'd say, "Well, do you got change for a ... ?"

"No, sir, I'll have to come back with the $5."

Then they would say, "No, just keep it. Just keep it."

By the time I would get through at 10 o'clock in the morning and get back to campus, I'd always have cash in my pocket. Best job I ever had because it always put money in my pocket.

YOU DO NOT CALL ANYBODY 'BOY'

The station where I worked as a DJ in college (originally KFRH, later KWUR) still exists. I know because I was at Washington University recently and stopped by to visit. When I worked there, it probably had just enough wattage to power a lamp. But it was a campus station like a lot of college radio stations, so that was really my first job in radio.

I don't even remember why I wanted to get into radio, but at first, I was doing a nighttime show where I'd play a little music and do a little talk. We certainly discussed civil rights at that time, but you've got to remember, the riots and affirmative action issues were relatively new concepts. So, we couldn't talk about anything real heavy because it was a college station.

I can barely remember who the young program director was, but even though he was just a college student, everything had to be done his way. He was always throwing orders around. That's the main thing I remember about him.

I think I ended up playing more music than I did anything else. Whatever music was hip at that time, I was playing it. It might have been the Fifth Dimension or Stax. Al Green was hot, the Four Tops, all of that. Obviously, I was into Motown because you've got to understand that Motown transcended everybody and everything. But I was at a white school playing Black music. And, if I'm not mistaken, I think I was on air for only an hour or two and I received no pay. That was really my first job in radio.

My football coach at Washington University was Richard Martin. He was the nicest white guy I had ever met. He was from Kansas City, Kansas, and just as country as he could be. He told me that they were in the process of building a strong athletic department and needed me because they were bringing in six freshmen from East St. Louis. (This was code for: "We've got some bad-ass street Negroes coming to a hostile campus.")

These young men were street-smart and had all attended a special program designed to get them out of the ghetto and into Washington University. When they got out on that football field, they were no-nonsense and would knock your head off. They played what we called "ghetto football." It was interesting because most of the white players came from prep schools, and the Black players would beat them up on the field badly.

Except for Shelby Jordan. He was 6'8", weighed 230 pounds and had never played football in his life. The coach saw this big Black kid walking on campus early in the year and assumed that he was part of the program, so he talked to him about tryouts. One day, Shelby was getting badly beaten up on the field. The white guys were picking on him because he was an easy target. I took Shelby aside, taught him a couple little tricks and a few techniques and told him, "If you don't kick they ass, I'm gon' kick your big ass." I also said, "You got some nerve letting these prep-school guys beat up on you. They're laughing at you and all that." The next thing I knew, Shelby was kicking their ass left and right and earned a starting position. Shelby went on to play for the Oakland Raiders.

The football coach had a graduate assistant, Chris John Gianoulakis, and when he would call out to the Black players on the field, he simply yelled, "Boy!" He was just a year or two removed from the fraternity house. One day, he said, "You boys down there, come here! You heard me!" I was at the other end of the field and watched the Black players (with that East St. Louis walk) walk up to him and say, "Who the fuck you calling boys?"

Gianoulakis responded, "Who do you all think you are talking to? I'm the coach around here! Give me five laps."

The players just stared him down and said, "We ain't going no fucking place!" I ran down the field and yelled to Coach Gianoulakis, "You see this piece of tape we got on our helmet? Those are our names. Why don't you just say Stewart, Cryder, Jordan, Madison? And if you can't read the names, just read the numbers?" I told him that you do not call anybody "boy." The civil rights movement had opened the door of higher education to low-income Black students who were not going to tolerate overt disrespect. This was the new attitude that my generation had developed by the late sixties.

As a teenager, I watched the Little Rock Nine and white mobs trying to prevent Vivian Jones from desegregating the University of Alabama and Charlayne Hunter-Gault from desegregating the University of Georgia. I was watching all of these young folks on television and remembered this exclusion had happened to me in Dayton and in Wisconsin. It was not overt. There was no one standing in front of the university preventing my admission. Still, I had to overcome the same marginalization that Black people all over the country were experiencing.

CHAPTER 3

WHO GAVE YOU PERMISSION TO CALL A BOYCOTT?

....

In 1971, I graduated from Washington University, returned to Dayton and worked six months in the communications department for Mead Corporation, having been recruited by Seymour Lundy, a Black public relations firm. Poverty, racism, and unemployment ignited riots in the late 1960s, and Black businesses were now receiving millions of dollars from the public and private sectors to hire Black employees. As Mead's director of urban affairs, I created projects to improve the image of local white banks in Black communities, enabling their managers to work alongside and build relationships with community members.

In 1973, Thomas Turner, the first Black president of the Detroit metropolitan AFL-CIO, invited me to work for the Detroit chapter of the National Association for the Advancement of Colored People (NAACP). He had been working in a steel factory and became a union leader around the same time Elliott Hall was elected president of the Detroit chapter of the NAACP. I think they might have learned about me through my work in Dayton. They initially invited me to a party in Detroit and surprised me by asking, "How would you like to run the

NAACP here?" We talked about the recruiting process, and I accepted the position.

At 24 years old, I was the youngest executive secretary of an NAACP branch ever, and I moved to Detroit. The work was not easy; the average age of our board members was 68, and the board consisted of current and former labor leaders, doctors, lawyers, teachers and principals. While the generation gap between the board and myself was evident from the get-go, I was young and ready to dive in. My first project was protesting Black exploitation films. During the 1970s, Hollywood financed a lot of Black films like "Super Fly" and "Foxy Brown." Men were generally portrayed as pimps and women as prostitutes; however, the movies did create jobs for Black actors. I invited Ron O'Neal — Super Fly himself — to Detroit to debate the issue of "blaxploitation" films, and I organized the NAACP youth to protest at movie theaters showing these films.

Some members of the NAACP were upset because I had their young people picketing theaters. I was surprised by this, since many of them used to stand in picket lines. I soon learned that a number of theater owners bought tickets to support our widely popular Freedom Fund dinner. They would call up and say things like, "We bought ads in the Freedom Fund dinner program, 10 tables, and you're out here picketing us? This guy you've got out here — y'all need to get him under control."

Also, there was a prostitution ring running rampant in the Black community; most of the johns were white male suburbanites. I started a campaign and got folks involved: Black people, churches, and white folk who lived in some of the affected neighborhoods and could not afford to move. However, I caught hell from the president of the Detroit chapter of the NAACP at the board meetings. The president said, "This has nothing to do with civil rights." I said, "But yes it does." He said, "No, it doesn't." I soon discovered that some of the lawyers on the NAACP board had represented some of the johns.

By the early 1970s, the auto industry was in a downward spiral, and as a result, many folks didn't have a lot of money. One of the major banks then announced that if accountholders had $50 or less in a savings account, they would close the account. In response, we encouraged African Americans to open savings accounts with Black-owned banks. This got a number of board members upset with me again. Many banks had purchased tickets to the Freedom Fund Dinner.

The last change I made (marking the end of my tenure as executive secretary of the Detroit chapter of the NAACP) was to the Freedom Fund Dinner itself. According to the *Guinness Book of World Records,* our annual Freedom Fund Dinner back then was the largest sit-down dinner in the world. The dinner, which provided funds to support the local branch programs, was held in Cobo Hall, had approximately 10,000 attendees, and charged $100 per plate.

Many people complained about the steak.

Serving 10,000 steaks was not easy; some steaks were cold, overcooked, and some folks wanted to place special orders. So I decided to change the menu; I asked my wife (who worked for United Airlines) to get a chef to volunteer to prepare the food. She got a bona fide four-star chef who worked for United Airlines, had a great reputation, and knew how to feed large groups of people. I asked him to put together a fabulous menu because people eat with their eyes; he suggested a chicken entrée. Our keynote speaker at the dinner was Carl Rowan, a Black journalist, and he appreciated the changes. He said, "This is the only place I know where thousands of people would pay $100 a plate to have chicken." However, at the next meeting with the Detroit NAACP executive officers, people screamed, "How dare you change the menu!" I said, "But wait a minute, we saved money because we didn't have to buy utensils, the chef volunteered his time, and we saved additional funds by going with chicken instead of expensive steaks." So, it was difficult. Even though I saved the organization money, there was hell to pay because I, again, didn't ask for permission from the board.

Around this time, I was also involved with the *Port Gibson v. NAACP* case. White merchants from the city of Port Gibson, Mississippi, sued the NAACP because the NAACP had called for a boycott of Port Gibson. The NAACP lost the first case, and in order to appeal, it had to pay double the judgment. This would have bankrupted the NAACP; however, that was really the whole purpose — to bankrupt us. The case ended up going to the United States Supreme Court and in the meantime, we raised money to cover court costs. I organized a telethon with absolutely no budget. We raised tens of thousands of dollars, and I got a number of Motown stars to perform, such as Bettye LaVette and Albert King of the Dramatics. This was a first for us, and the money came pouring in. For once, nobody said anything. In this case, silence was truly golden; everyone was very happy. Still, I realized that working as the executive secretary of the Detroit branch of the NAACP was not my long-term goal. I wanted to be a civil rights activist.

Not surprisingly, many of my older colleagues did not support this.

After I lived in Detroit for three years, I decided to run for city council. There were nine at-large seats with seven incumbents, so there were only two open seats. I received over 113,000 votes and finished 13th. Ken Cockrel, a militant Black attorney of the people, won. He was to Detroit what Johnnie Cochran was to Southern California; he took on numerous police brutality cases and developed an excellent reputation. He barely squeaked into the ninth position.

In 1977, Benjamin Hooks hired me as political director of the NAACP. He had been recently elected president of the NAACP; had two large churches (the Greater Mount Mariah in Detroit and his home church in Memphis, Tennessee); was a judge; and was the first Black on the Federal Communications Commission. He asked me if I wanted to be the political director of the NAACP and join his national staff. He wanted to relocate the NAACP offices from Birmingham to Detroit because voter registration drives were focusing on the South and the North was suffering. In fact, there was a great deal of apathy in the North.

I accepted the position and remained in Detroit. I was running for executive director at the same time he was running for national office. I knew they were just putting me in there so they could say they had a young person; however, they asked me to submit my resume so they could also say they had done a legitimate search. They even hired a search firm but to be honest, it was all just a front. With the NAACP, they make up their minds, the votes are counted, and the person is already in.

In 1985, some people from Detroit wanted to picnic in neighboring Dearborn. However, some white Dearborn residents came up to the Black folks and said, "This is our park and you're from Detroit." They told them they had to leave. In Dearborn at the time, if you were Black, you had to be out by dark and couldn't go back before dawn. If you did, the police would stop you and say you had to have a letter from your employer. The Black folk complained to the Dearborn City Council and the mayor, but the council had already passed an ordinance stating that only residents of Dearborn could use its public parks.

Dearborn actually had one of the largest predominantly Black local unions because the Ford Motor Company had relocated there. So Black folk worked in Dearborn; they just didn't live there. Art Featherstone, a militant who worked for Rep. John Conyers of Michigan, said, "Joe, we gotta do something about it."

So, on Thanksgiving Eve, I took a page from the demonstrations at the South African Embassy. Rosa Parks (who was also working for Conyers) and I agreed to hold a news conference and announce that we were going to boycott the city of Dearborn. We encouraged all Detroit residents not to shop or spend a dime in Dearborn, which, for starters, had a large shopping mall called Fairlane Mall. We said, "If we can't play in your parks, we're not going to pay in your stores." We started on Thanksgiving because it's generally a slow news day. So we got a big headline: Rosa Parks and Joe Madison announce boycotting the entire city of Dearborn — don't buy gas, go to the mall or do anything in Dearborn. The reaction was instantaneous, and sales in Dearborn collapsed as Black people stopped going there.

The Friday after Thanksgiving is, of course, Black Friday, which is one of the key shopping days in the U.S. every year. So we were riding high. Debates soon erupted; Dearborn civic leaders wanted us to leave town. They insisted that they could take care of their own issues. They said, "White folks and Black folks get along, so why are you all boycotting? We don't have to boycott. We can work this out." Also, Henry Ford II was pissed. He called Mayor Coleman Young and told him to shut me down.

But we kept going.

NBC's "Today Show" began covering the boycott, which was similar to the boycott in Birmingham; it was almost like what King had experienced. I'll never forget a meeting with Marc Stepp, vice president of United Auto Workers (UAW), which was the largest majority-Black union at the time; Damon Keith, a federal judge; and Buddy Battle — these were the movers and shakers in Detroit, and they were Young's kitchen cabinet. Every Saturday morning, they met for breakfast over scrambled eggs and bourbon. They asked me to come join them one Saturday, and then they chewed my ass out.

They said, "How dare you call a boycott without our permission? Who gave you permission to call a boycott?"

I said, "I didn't think I need anybody's permission to call a boycott."

Mayor Young shouted, "You're in my city. How dare you! I got Henry Ford calling me. You should have come to us." It got so bad that they forbade me from being interviewed on the "Today Show." They wanted

Rev. Charles Adams to do it; Adams was the president of the Detroit Chapter of the NAACP and, of course, didn't support the boycott.

Young and his kitchen cabinet soon cut a deal; Henry Ford asked Dearborn to rescind its ordinance and instead fight it out in the state court. Ford and Young agreed. Now, Conyers was in favor of the boycott and knew Dearborn had received federal money. He said, "How are they going tell Detroit residents that they can't use their parks?" This ordinance clearly targeted Blacks. They might as well have said, "We don't want y'all in our parks, and we don't want you playing basketball."

We had another meeting with Bob King, a white man and president of the UAW. King had a meeting scheduled with Horace Sheffield Jr., who was a retired UAW official. They invited me to the meeting at Union Hall. King stood up and said, "You can't call a boycott without my permission. This is my town. What do you mean telling my UAW members that they can't stop and buy gas?"

After he made that statement, I lost it. I said, "Let me tell you something! Until your mama, your sister, or somebody in your family is told they can't even go to a damn park because of the color of their skin, you ain't in no fucking position to tell me I can't call a boycott to protect the rights of people to go anywhere in this damn country they want to go. You can kiss my ass." As I walked out of the meeting, someone said, "Call the boycott off." I said, "I'm not going to call off the boycott; I'm not going do it."

Even after the Black leaders called off the boycott, I maintained my position of not ending it until the court case was decided. However, that year, Henry Ford decided to pay for the entire 10,000 guests at the Freedom Fund Dinner as well as the event's overhead, so I lost a lot of needed support. Nevertheless, the "Today Show" producers called me to debate the mayor of Dearborn. I also got a call from Joe Davis, the civil rights director of the UAW. He asked me to come to a meeting in his office and then made me wait for an hour. He told me that Mayor Young did not want me to go on the "Today Show;" as a matter of fact, none of these people wanted me to go on the "Today Show" because of the agreement they made with Ford.

The case was headed to the Michigan Supreme Court. and Rev. Adams' name was on the lawsuit and not mine because the "Black leaders" had co-opted it. They told me to call the "Today Show" and tell them that Rev. Adams would talk about the case. I said, "I'm not going to recommend Rev. Adams to go on no damn "Today Show." First of all, it ain't up to me, it's up to the producers of the "Today Show." " Davis told me that if I went on the "Today Show," I would never work in the city of Detroit again and, given Mayor Young's influence around the country, I would never work anywhere else in the country either.

I said, "You're threatening my livelihood! You're threatening my ability to make a living for my family!" I wanted to kick his ass right then and there; we really had it out, and it almost came to blows. I told him, "You can tell Coleman Young to kiss my ass." So I went on the "Today Show," did the debate, held my own, and then we waited on the ruling by the Michigan Supreme Court.

A few days after my "Today Show" interview, I attended a late-night meeting at Adams' church. Arthur Johnson and Judge Damon Keith were there, and they asked Ben Hooks to come and bring me with him. We got there, and they told Ben, "We want him out of town. He's just uncontrollable. He doesn't need to be here. I don't care where you take him, just take him out of here."

We were sitting in the pews of an empty church in the middle of the night. Hooks politely listened and then said, "You know, I've been through boycotts with Dr. King; I know that boycotts are successful, and this one has been successful. That's why y'all got me here. 'Cause if it wasn't successful, y'all wouldn't have me here." He added, "There's only two ways boycotts are successful — they're either spontaneous or they're well-organized. This was a spontaneous reaction to institutional racism in the city of Dearborn, and I ain't taking this man nowhere. Come on, Joe, we're leaving."

We got up and walked out of the church. I'll never forget that meeting. The Michigan Supreme Court ended up ruling in our favor. On the front page of the *Detroit News* is a picture of Art Featherstone, another guy and myself, and we are cracking up. We looked like hyenas because we had just received the news that the court had ruled in our favor, declaring the city ordinance unconstitutional.

I really came of age during this time and now considered myself a professional activist. However, the boycott did take a toll on my personal life. Activists have to balance their personal and political commitments, but I was still in my early 20s at the time. My wife and I divorced, and my parents and grandparents all died.

Years later, I attended the Democratic National Convention, saw Bob

King, and smiled, but he ignored me. I learned that these guys stake out a position and you are either on their side or you are not. Playing both sides from the middle is not appreciated. They also test you. Young told me that he was pissed because I did not have the sense to join his administration; I told him I didn't work for politicians. He offered government jobs to all the young "rabble rousers" back then, and the benefits and security made it very difficult to refuse. He offered me a job that paid three times my salary at the time, and it would have made me the "unofficial" mayor of my neighborhood; however, I had just applied for the position of executive secretary with the national NAACP organization.

I had long thought Damon Keith couldn't stand my guts; he was the federal judge who challenged Nixon when he was wiretapping everybody. Recently, I ran into him in Washington, D.C., at the 50th anniversary of the *Brown v. Board of Education* ruling. I hadn't seen him since I left Detroit. After the event, he came up to me, grabbed me and hugged my wife. He said, "You know, man, you're something else; you've come a long way." So I realized that these guys, they go to battle, and sometimes they battle each other. But if you're strong and have the courage of your convictions, they respect you. Now, they may try to kick your ass, but they will respect you. However, if you're weak, they won't have anything to do with you. They endured their own trials and respect others who have done the same.

MY ROOTS IN RADIO

I first worked in radio when I was in college at Washington University in St. Louis. At the time, they had a little college station with as much power as a hairdryer; I wasn't sure if students even bothered to listen. We didn't do talk radio; we just played music. When I first started talk radio, there were very few Black radio talk show hosts to emulate; however, I got the opportunity to learn from one of the best. Mark Scott was one of the most influential radio talk show personalities at the time. Our political views were quite different, but he didn't care, and he helped me out enormously. I quickly adopted his style; he jumped all over callers who failed to substantiate their positions. He was a voracious reader so when callers acted like fools, he ripped their arguments apart. I'm the same way; I don't want anyone calling my show, acting like a fool and underestimating me.

My first talk show radio job was with a public affairs show produced by WCHB, a Black station. I worked on weekends; the show covered the activities of the NAACP. My radio career began during the infamous 1974 *Milliken v. Bradley* Supreme Court case, which addressed crosstown busing. The NAACP asked me to debate a lawyer who was anti-busing.

During this period, talk radio shows had to have representatives from both sides of the debate. I held my own during the debate and afterwards, Michael Packer, the program director of WXYZ (home of the Lone Ranger and the Green Hornet) talked to me about a weekend spot on Saturday and Sunday. He said, "Would you like to do talk radio?" I said, "Sure, but I've never done radio other than some college radio and a public affairs show that I had with the NAACP." This was when talk radio was just coming into its own.

I ended up working weekends for the next decade. This was a conservative station, and I soon discovered that no matter how good I was, I was not going to get an opportunity to work during the week. The station's manager hired white people to work primetime slots even though they sometimes lacked talk radio experience altogether. The station's owners gave Denny McLain, a former pitcher for the Detroit Tigers who had just gotten out of prison, a morning talk show. He had no experience and burned out quickly. Initially people would call in because they were excited to talk one-on-one with Denny, a World Series hero and former Cy Young winner; however, after a year or two, his star began to fade.

Successful talk show hosts learn the trade, understand their audiences and develop their own personalities. It's not about whether listeners like or dislike you; the objective is that they want to hear what you have to say. This is what has served me well — I decide who I want to be and what I want to talk about, and I remain true to that. Also, you can make an honest mistake, and people will forgive you, but you should not try to be someone you are not. Some talk show hosts pretend to be conservative or liberal just because they think that's what the audience wants to hear, but listeners see right through it.

My show examined politics in Detroit, and I continued my activism with the NAACP. The majority of my guests were local elected officials, county officials and some entertainers. One of the most important issues back then was AIDS and HIV. During the outbreak of the AIDS epidemic, I realized that most people were ignorant and did not understand the AIDS virus. I was one of the first hosts at the station to interview someone with AIDS. After the show, the engineer came in, took the microphone used by the guest, and threw it away. You are talking about an expensive piece of equipment; this really showed me how ignorant and paranoid folks were about AIDS. I took a number of calls from people who believed that AIDS was a manmade biological disease. That discussion went on for several years.

In addition to serious political topics, I interviewed a number of famous entertainers, including the Temptations and Captain Kangaroo. Captain Kangaroo was actually one of my most popular interviews. I discovered that he was a war veteran, and we did not talk about his dancing bear. I talked to him outside, and we drew a large crowd that day because everyone wanted to see him. Now, when I interview people, I always try to find out who they are. Captain Kangaroo was not Captain Kangaroo all of his life. So I asked him, "What were you before you were Captain Kangaroo?" He gave a lengthy discussion about his participation in the war and the impact that it had on him. He was a peacenik; that's how he got into children's programming. He was a very nice man and very political; he was a liberal who supported public education.

Our station had a suburban, predominantly white audience, so the majority of the talk show hosts had topics that interested white suburbanites. I was the only Black on-air personality who lived in Detroit. Interestingly, the station refused to allow Mayor Young to be a guest on my show. He asked me why, and I told him, "Because they're paying me." Nevertheless, I tried to educate suburban whites about Mayor Young and Detroit politics. Many callers referred to Young in racist language, and some white listeners said I was a racist like him. Some callers said Young was destroying Detroit, and I was just a mouthpiece for Coleman Young. But if you criticized Young for something he did, Black people called in and said, "You're an Uncle Tom, and how can you be out there in that station criticizing our first Black mayor?"

I got my first break to do a full-time talk radio show in Philadelphia. The overnight shift was from midnight to 5:30 in the morning at WWDB, which was a talk station. Once again, I was the only Black person on the air. Since it was during the week, I kept my weekend job in Detroit;

however, I moved my family to Philadelphia since I was there five days a week.

I was in Philadelphia for less than 90 days before Diane Raymond, the program director, and Charles Schwartz, the owner, called me in and said, "We're getting letters that you're a racist. You can't talk about Black people as long as you're on the air." I said, "What do you mean I can't talk about Black folk?" This was a couple years after the bombing on Osage Avenue in 1985; the neighborhood was still smoldering. Of course, during the day, white folks discussed Black folks all the time and constantly criticized Mayor Wilson Goode (who is Black). And I said, "You know what, this is bullshit."

So, the next day I arranged to interview Louis Farrakhan of the Nation of Islam. In other words, fuck 'em. But I'm going to be cool. So I interviewed Farrakhan for one hour and the next hour I interviewed my good friend Ron Brown, who was running to be the first Black chairman of the Democratic National Committee. I wanted to show the dichotomy of the Black community through these two interviews. But the next day, they called me in and fired me.

They said, "We found out that you've been traveling back to Detroit on weekends and doing your weekend show and that's a conflict of interest."

I said, "Wait a minute. It's my weekend."

"Well, we would have preferred you to stay in the city on the weekends so you could have gotten to know the city."

I said, "Then I'd prefer you pay me to stay here on the weekends. You're not paying me for Saturdays and Sunday. I get off Friday morning at 5:30."

They said, "Well, it's a conflict."

I said, "You've got a guy in Baltimore who is driving to Philadelphia to do his show."

They fired me anyway.

This is how I ended up at WWRC in Washington. During the interview, I must've been crazy at the time. I told the committee, "I've been through this before; I'm not taking Bev Smith's place." She was a Black female radio talk show host, and I did not want to be part of replacing one Black person with another. I said, "So if that's what you're trying to do, you can keep the job. I refuse to be the only Black boy on radio because you fired Bev Smith."

"Oh, why would you think we would do that?" the interviewer said.
I said, "I told you, I've been through this before."
So they didn't do that, but eventually Bev left.

During the audition for the WWRC position in Washington D.C., I learned a great lesson in talk radio. The program director had a little button inside the control room so phone calls could not get through. He did not tell you this during the audition. He wanted to see if I could be engaging for half an hour. Anybody can light up phone lines and oftentimes that's how stations grade success (by the number of lines that are lit). All I had to do was talk about hot topics such as race, religion, abortion or gun control, and the lines would light up. Like my grandfather said, "Opinions are like assholes, everybody's got one."

The fact of the matter is that over 90 percent of your listeners never call talk radio; they just listen. This was why the program director had hit the button; he wanted to see if I could carry a conversation on my own. The most successful talk show hosts are the ones who know what they are talking about. This is one reason why Rev. Al Sharpton is so good; he only talks about what he knows. He has had experiences so he can tell his listeners, "Let me tell you about this and let me tell you about that, because I was there." When talk show hosts talk about information that they don't know, that's when they get into trouble. That's why Don Imus got into trouble referring to the Black women on the Rutgers University Women's basketball as "nappy-headed hos." He was trying to be funny and did not know a damn thing about how sensitive the Black community is to such an affront.

Talk radio gave me a platform to express my views, but I noticed that, like everywhere else in the United States, there is a double standard in the talk radio industry. One day I started talking about religion and the Virgin Mary. I said, "Well, there's some folk that just don't buy it; some people think that Mary might've gotten knocked up." My program director called me to his office and suspended me for a week because I was not allowed to say that the Virgin Mary got knocked up. This was the mid-eighties and Howard Stern was on the air saying whatever he wanted. So there's always a double standard. White guys can say anything about Black men and women. Rush Limbaugh and other conservative talk show hosts get away with racist and sexist comments. Can you imagine telling one of the few Black talk show hosts in the city of Philadelphia, a year or two after the MOVE bombing, that I could not talk about Black folks in a city that was so racially divided?

When I started working in talk radio, I had to follow the Fairness Doctrine. All talk show hosts had to present both sides of an issue. If I interviewed a conservative, I had to interview a liberal. For example, when the local station asked me to debate the *Milliken v. Bradley* case, I supported one side and a lawyer supported the other. We would be in the studio together and have an honest debate; however, once the stations eliminated the Fairness Doctrine, all talk show hosts had to do is give one side. This is why you now have entire right-wing radio stations.

The individuals behind the elimination of the Fairness Doctrine were Mitt Romney types: wealthy, male and conservative. Members of the Cox family in Atlanta are conservative Democrats; however, they put right-wing reactionary Republicans on the air who oppose public education, Medicare, unions and affirmative action, and who attract plenty of listeners who agree with their positions. With that kind of history, how can you then add a liberal at that station and expect that person to survive? It's like having an R&B station and then playing Willie Nelson. What's going to happen? You are going to get phone calls, and they are going to say, "What the hell is wrong with you?" That's how the game works. Now, people say, "The only reason there aren't any liberal stations is because conservatives make up the bulk of the listeners." No, that's not true. It's that people are fed one ideology to the point that they don't think there's any other.

Liberal talk radio has tried to compete with conservative talk; for example, Al Gore's Air America was a feeble attempt to challenge right-wing talk, but they did not hire authentic talk show talent. For example, they hired Chuck D from Public Enemy. If they did a show on how to be a rapper, Chuck D would have been authentic. They next hired Al Franken, a writer for "Saturday Night Live" and a future senator from Minnesota. Franken had never hosted a talk show but he used that as a platform to run for the U.S. Senate and got paid a fortune because his name was on the marquee. Callers got to say, "Oh, I got to talk to Al Franken." Well, that gets old after a while. I'm not saying Chuck D and Al Franken could not become good talk show hosts; however, the reality is that if a station does not hire trained talk show personalities, it will fail.

During the 1980s, African American voter registration in the North was low. Growing up in Ohio and living in Michigan, I was familiar with the Underground Railroad and Harriet Tubman; the Underground Railroad, of course, was a group of trails that led from the Southern part of the United States to the North and Canada. I was aware of the paths that ran from Kentucky to Michigan and into Canada.

Since African Americans in the North needed to increase their voter registration and participation, I came up with a concept called the "Overground Railroad" in 1983. We began in Louisville, Kentucky, followed the path of the Underground Railroad, and registered people to vote in each of the cities that we passed. Before the march, I identified the local NAACP branches along the route, and the majority of our volunteers were NAACP youth members and adults. Our march received a great deal of publicity, because we had approximately 100 marchers. Our motto was, we would go overground to guarantee our freedom by voting, the way that our ancestors went underground. This was why we called it the Overground Railroad March. We marched through Cincinnati, Dayton, and Columbus. We would spend the day marching, register voters in the evening and spend the night. The next day, we would get up and start marching at five o'clock in the morning. We walked 15 to 25 miles a day. Our final day of marching culminated in Detroit, where we had a big rally.

The Canadian government invited the marchers to march across the border. After the rally, many of the marchers went to Canada to see where the slaves had traveled. The march was very successful, and it focused a lot of attention on voter registration. Weeks after the march, we started getting requests from other regions in the country. So, we conducted another Overground Railroad March, from Richmond, Virginia, to New York City.

After this march, folks out West said they needed to increase the number of registered voters. So we walked from San Francisco to Los Angeles, during Jesse Jackson's first presidential campaign. He was campaigning in an area not too far behind us; after we marched, he would arrive in a city, give a speech, and received all of the publicity because he was running for president. However, we were registering all of the voters. He claims that he registered many of those voters, and to this day Reverend Al still laughs about it. People in Jesse's camp knew we were registering voters. However, we could not do it on behalf of

Jesse Jackson because we were non-partisan. We had to be very cautious. For example, on some days, we would be in the same city as Jackson, and my marchers were young and often wanted to attend his rallies. I told them Ben Hooks was concerned about the NAACP losing its tax-exempt status if its members were viewed as Jackson supporters. More importantly, we did not want Jackson to co-opt our movement.

During our marches, we registered voters, got them engaged, and received financial support from politicians and entertainers. Aretha Franklin was a major financial supporter of our march. When we marched up the East Coast through Delaware, Sen. Joseph Biden was a huge supporter of our marches. Sherrod Brown, a senator from Ohio, also walked with us from Columbus, Ohio. During our West Coast march, Wally Amos Jr. of Famous Amos cookies marched with us. In 1984, I organized a voter-registration march from Los Angeles to Baltimore, joined by the same group of people who had marched with us before.

We did not walk through the Mojave Desert; we took the southern route. This march took a great deal of planning because we had to notify all the NAACP branches in Arizona and Nevada. When we stopped in Las Vegas, Bill Cosby invited us to his show at Caesars Palace, and he took photographs with everybody backstage and gave us a contribution.

In 1984, the anti-apartheid movement started to pick up momentum. A growing number of protesters focused on the South African government's racist policies. During the summer, I organized this march from Los Angeles to Baltimore with the intention of arriving in Baltimore during the NAACP national convention. When we traveled into a city, we were generally served fried chicken in a church. The kids cracked jokes because at every stop, Black women in white dresses always served us fried chicken; the marchers learned to look for the sisters in the white dresses because they knew that they were going to get some good food. We often slept in churches, people's homes and school gymnasiums.

The march provided opportunities for activists of all ages and generations to form lifelong bonds. Our youngest marchers were 16, and one of our oldest marchers was 72 years old: Mr. Jim Ramsey. We met Mr. Ramsey in Oklahoma, and he was one of our best marchers because he was a senior marathon runner. The young guys were really cocky college kids — Morehouse types — and they would challenge each other in order to break the monotony of the march. One day, the college students challenged Mr. Ramsey to a race and he ran those kids tongue thin.

During our cross-country march, we asked people to sign petitions for the Senate opposing apartheid in South Africa. We marched from Mississippi to Arkansas; up the East Coast through the Carolinas; and into Baltimore during the NAACP national convention. We presented tens of thousands of signatures to Sen. Charles Mathias, who was chairman of the Foreign Affairs Committee and was spearheading an anti-apartheid bill in Congress. So, our march had a dual purpose; we registered voters, and people signed anti-apartheid petitions. For this reason, we called this a march for human dignity.

I served as the national NAACP political director for six years. During our summer march, I discovered that the NAACP's executive board had created a new board position that convention delegates would elect. I decided to run for that seat, though I was still director of the political action department and staff members could not run for the board. Therefore, I had to resign before I ran, but Ben Hooks refused to accept my resignation.

Hooks held a personnel committee meeting, and Judge Charles V. Johnson from Seattle and I were both on the panel. The committee called on me to make a case. They told me that staff people should not be allowed to run. However, Judge Johnson said, "Ben, he has resigned. Did you receive the letter on time?" Ben said, "Yes." Judge Johnson said, "Then, I'm just gonna tell you like it is, you can hire him when you want to, but you can't tell that young man he can't quit. You can't do it." And the committee voted to accept my letter of resignation.

I ran an intense campaign. It was like running for president. I had flyers, balloons, and my key advantage was I had just walked across the country so I was kind of a celebrity, and there was tons of buzz. The other advantage was that 25 of the core marchers worked for my campaign. So I was elected to the NAACP board and held that position for 14 years. I was the 65th board member.

My position was key because there was so much internal politics on the board. During my campaign, Hooks actually had his board members campaign against me. They were presidents of the NAACP state conferences and tried to persuade the delegates from different states, "Don't vote for Joe. Don't vote for Joe." But in spite of him and his supporters, I won. After my nomination, Hooks passed the Madison rule — no staff person could run for the board until they have been off the staff for at least two years.

During my first decade of talk radio, I combined my civil rights activism with my radio talk show. So I brought my experience from the street into the studio. When someone called in and started telling me about what the NAACP is not doing, I reminded them that I was on the national board and had served as the national political director. On numerous occasions, callers told me, "Jesse Jackson did this and Jesse Jackson said that." Again, I had to remind them, "Whoa, whoa, excuse me. I was there, and I just had lunch with Jesse Jackson."

So I shared my perspective and experiences with my audience. I worked for the NAACP and was trained in the civil rights movement. I understood the civil rights movement better than my listeners and provided a perspective that they did not have. I was marching and protesting for most of my professional career. This does not mean I do not respect my audience's opinion but when they say anything that is inaccurate about the NAACP or civil rights activism, I set the record straight.

Another on-air hurdle was learning to talk about race to whites during the 1980s. Ronald Reagan and the Republican Party had created political, economic and social programs that devastated Black communities. For example, the War on Drugs was really a war on young Black and Latino drug users and low-level dealers that created prison industrial complexes. In 1981, Reagan fired striking air traffic controllers and U.S. union membership started to decline. White flight, double-digit unemployment and rising crime rates were rampant in Frost Belt cities such as Detroit and Philadelphia. In addition, Reagan was anti-affirmative action, anti-busing, and he supported apartheid in South Africa. The overwhelming majority of whites believed that Black folk were the root cause of all these problems, and I had to present a whole different story.

Radio talk show is a misnomer. Talk radio has existed for a long time, but call-in talk radio emerged during the 1980s as a vehicle for people to express their opinions. Americans grew up listening to the Ed Murrow and Mike Wallace shows; however, they did all of the talking and did not take calls from listeners. This is the difference between talk radio and call-in talk radio — you listened but could not call. I began my radio career during the early days of call-in and talk, call-in and debate, call-in and argue radio.

As social transformations were happening around the country, a number of whites would call in to debate various issues. As I said earlier, successful talk show hosts are honest with their listeners. From day one, I let my audience know that I was going to give them a Black perspective because the Black perspective has always been undervalued, underestimated and marginalized. I tried to legitimize it and show folk how my (Black) history is your U.S. history; you can't separate the two. Moreover, my perspective is just as important as your perspective. You have a perspective as a white suburbanite, and I have a perspective as an urban Black. Now, sometimes there are going to be differences, but in many cases, there are going to be similarities. For example, you want an affordable education for your child, and I want an affordable education for my child. You want good health care, and I want good health care. You want a good job, and I want a good job. We do not have to be at odds with each other.

It is difficult to measure your impact on your audience. The best measurement of my show is that people really appreciate my honesty. I will always get people who call in and say, "I don't agree with you 90 percent of the time," but they still listen to me because I am educating them. So even though they disagree, they are listening. Sometimes the audience is tuning in just to disagree with you; however, I walk a fine line. I feel that it is my obligation to provide the counter voice to both conservative talk and liberal talk, which also marginalizes and sanitizes the Black perspective.

As a talk show host, I try to remain informed and never be caught short on facts. I have to do the research and always know what I'm talking about. If I am not familiar with a topic, I try to avoid discussing it on air. Still, mistakes do happen and before the internet, I could get away with it. But I try to read 10 to 15 newspapers a day, and my real strength is that I was an active participant in many of the events that I now discuss. Most on-air personalities have spent their entire careers in a studio — a padded soundproof room behind a microphone. I have an insider's perspective that my colleagues don't necessarily have. I'm fond of saying, "I didn't develop my craft in a padded room behind a microphone."

CHAPTER 4

HELLUVA PLACE TO DO RADIO

Even before I was fired a few times, my path into radio had been somewhat circuitous.

In 1987, I lost my first full-time radio gig in Philadelphia and thought my radio career was over before it even began. I had just relocated my entire family, my wife had just found new work, and my employer fired me just before the 90-day period. So I did some fill-in work, trying to keep my name out there.

I got invited to do Geraldo Rivera's television show; the topic was the emergence of talk radio. This was when Geraldo was a Latino liberal; the question was why WABC in New York didn't have a Black person on the radio. An audience member called in and said, "You do have a Black person on. Someone named Charlie Jones."

Geraldo said, "Oh yeah, I forgot about him. But we don't think of him as being Black."

Well, man, that just opened up all kinds of doors and opportunities for discussion. The debate got heated and fortunately for me, in the audience was the program director for WWRC in Washington. The producers of the Geraldo show had invited him to be an in-studio guest, and he heard me. He called me the next day and said, "Look, if they don't want you in Philadelphia, we want you in Washington. We want you to come to D.C. right away and be on the air."

The night I came to Washington, D.C., after being dismissed in Philadelphia, I unpacked my clothes in my hotel room. Not two or three blocks away was the Vista Hotel, where former Washington Mayor Marion Barry was arrested. And that's how come I always remember that day, Jan. 18, 1990.

It was a circus.

I was supposed to go the next day to Annapolis and appear on a show to debate abortion rights at the Maryland State Legislature, but I turned on the TV and Marion Barry was getting arrested just two blocks away.

So my brand-new program director at WRC called me. Forget the Annapolis show, he said, I was now going to the courthouse to cover the mayor's arraignment, to do interviews outside the courthouse. It was a zoo — every station, every network was out there.

They had arranged to have a mobile talk studio for me. OK, it was really just a converted van. We would interview people on the street throughout the D.C. metropolitan area. They called me "The Man in the Van."

It was then I realized that D.C. was going to be one helluva place to do talk radio.

THE SHOOTING OF ARTIE ELLIOTT

The Black Lives Matter movement has suddenly made police brutality against Black people a central issue in America. But of course it's hardly a new problem.

Back in 1993, Archie "Artie" Elliott III, a young Black man, was driving home from his construction job in District Heights, Maryland, on a Friday when he stopped to have a few beers. Two police officers, Jason Leavitt and Wayne Cheney, pulled him over afterward on suspicion of drunken driving. It was a hot day, so he was wearing nothing but a pair of shorts and tennis shoes — he didn't even have on socks or a shirt. The police determined that he was intoxicated, so they searched him, handcuffed him, put him in the front seat of the squad car and strapped him in. But the two police officers, both of them Black, said Artie Elliott managed to pull a gun and pointed it at them, so the officers fired 22 times, hitting Elliott 14 times in the chest, arms, hand and elsewhere.

By the time we got to the case there had already been a trial, and the police officers were exonerated. As I often say on the radio, the only thing that's new is that which is forgotten.

Not surprisingly, Elliott's mother came to us because she felt the prosecutor had not done the right thing in prosecuting the police — just like in Ferguson, Missouri. Prince George's County, where this occurred, was a predominantly Black county outside of Washington, D.C. So, I began talking about it on the radio, and interviewed his mother and relatives. This story became an issue on the radio. I had a meeting with the prosecutor, Jack Johnson, where I asked him if he would reopen the case. That is what the mother was trying to do — get the case re-opened. So, he started pontificating about how if he had been the prosecutor at the time, he would reopen the case.

I said, "Well, you are the prosecutor. You can reopen this case."

He said, "You know what, I think I might. I think that's something I'm going to consider doing."

Of course, I get on the air, saying, "Oh, you know, we may be able to...."

Johnson then denies we ever had that conversation. Well, man, I decided we were going to picket his office. So every Wednesday at noon after I got off the air, we would go out to the county courthouse and picket his office.

People from Baltimore, Prince George's County and Washington, D.C., came out and picketed. We did this for weeks. Then we would get arrested for acts of civil disobedience. We were joined by Radio One's FM personalities, comedian George Wallace and Les Brown, along with Martin Luther King III and Dick Gregory. Folks started coming in from across the country.

Then we did a march from Prince George's County to Annapolis, 22 miles away, so it was one mile for every bullet. We even asked the governor to appoint a special prosecutor, but we were unsuccessful. I ended up being sued by the two police officers for defamation of character. Why? Because on the air I had said they murdered Artie Elliott.

We went to court, and our attorney for Radio One said Cathy Hughes, founder and majority owner of the radio network, was with me the whole way. She never said, "Don't do it." She was right there. Even though she never showed up at any marches or anything, she never pulled the plug on it. I did have a vice president from Radio One who got nervous.

He said, "Well, Joe, come on, he's the district attorney, man. Why are you doing this?"

He was nervous because we were based in Prince George's County, so he was thinking about our business relationships there, tax issues, and all that. But Cathy Hughes and her son Alfred Liggins III, president of the network, never told me to back off. Never.

We ended up in court and the judge dismissed the case. The lesson I learned was that it came down to whether there was an intent to defame. I had used the word "murder," and the attorney said all I had to do was say "kill." Some killings can be justified, but murder cannot. So the attorney said, "That's how we're gonna explain it to the court. Your intent was not to defame them, you were just describing what happened. You have the First Amendment right to talk about what happened."

So the case was dismissed. But the whole family was on pins and needles because I never knew what the cops looked like, never met them. There was always this concern that I might be a target.

The case drew national attention and was a forerunner to Ferguson, Missouri. And here's the irony: The Black ministers tried to crucify me. But I had the support of the Black leaders who mattered. Members of Walter Fauntroy's New Bethel Baptist Church in Washington, D.C., marched with me, and Bishop C. Anthony Muse, a state senator, had his church come out and march as well. People would take the bus from Baltimore and come down to march.

So we decided we were going to have a meeting with Jack Johnson and what amounted to his religious supporters, and one of them was a guy I went to college with. Unfortunately, Fauntroy ended up going out of the country, so I had to meet with them separately.

But some of the other ministers raked me across the coals, pissed that Fauntroy wasn't there.

They said, "Well, why isn't he here? He's not good enough to be here? We took our time to be here."

I said, "Look, Fauntroy's in Africa somewhere. I'm here."

It turned out to be a setup. Jack Johnson was running for county executive and that's why his supporters were mad — this was bringing him negative attention. Eventually he won and became county executive, but God don't like ugly. In the end, Johnson was busted by the FBI for extortion and taking bribes — both he and his wife, Leslie, who was on the county council.

So the story goes, his wife calls him on the phone.

"The FBI agents are at the door. What should I do with the money?"

He says, "Stuff it in your bra and your panties."

All the while, the FBI is listening to him over a wiretapped line tell his wife: "The money's downstairs. Go get it."

When they arrest her, she has wads of money stuffed in her panties and her bra.

That's the wife of the same man who refused to reopen the Artie Elliott case. Both he and his wife were sent to prison. In 2011, he was sentenced to 87 months in prison, had to pay a $100,000 fine, and was forced to forfeit $78,000 and an antique Mercedes-Benz.

So, once again, I ended up on the right side. Meanwhile, not one of those ministers has ever come and said, "You know what, you were right."

This is why you have to be careful and do due diligence on every story. You've got to make sure everything is right, and you've got to make sure people are telling you the truth. And when you are successful at taking on tough cases, people come out of the woodwork and will ask, "Will you take my case?"

I can't tell you how many legal folders and court documents I get. Sometimes cases are in binders that people send, begging, "Please read this case and I need your help."

I'm not a lawyer; I'm not a law firm. I don't have a bank of lawyers. And I feel bad because sometimes I can't decipher what I'm reading. And 90 percent of the time you have to say no, because that's not really your job. But people need help and they still turn to you because sometimes you're the only voice out there. Maybe they have turned to the NAACP, or Rev. Sharpton, or this source or that source. But a lot of times you're the only place they have to go to. It's sad. It weighs on you because some folks legitimately need help.

I even had the white former governor of Alabama, Don Siegelman, turn to me for help. He was convicted on federal felony corruption charges in 2006 and sentenced to seven years in federal prison. He believed he was railroaded. I knew him when he was the lieutenant governor of Alabama. He was the last Democrat to be elected governor of Alabama.

So, it's not just Black folk. It's just not local people. Here was a governor who was indicted, tried, convicted and sent to federal prison. Now, I do believe he was railroaded for political purposes, and we tried to help. He was released from prison on Feb. 8, 2017.

'DARK ALLIANCE,' THE CIA AND THE CRACK EPIDEMIC

Then there was the situation with Gary Webb.

In the summer of 1996, while I was doing talk radio with WRC, I get a call from somebody who said, "Have you read the *Mercury* newspaper?"

The San Jose Mercury News — a respected major regional paper in the heart of Silicon Valley — had just run a series called "Dark Alliance," written by reporter Gary Webb, that focused on the crack cocaine epidemic and its origins in Los Angeles, drug dealer "Freeway" Ricky Ross, and the connections between the CIA, Oliver North and the Contras in Nicaragua. I had not read it, so I started reading. Right after I read the series, I got on the phone and started calling different people, particularly on the West Coast. I called all the contacts I could, including the head of the NAACP and members of the Congressional Black Caucus. The problem was that everybody was at the Democratic National Convention that year in Chicago.

I called Dick Gregory and I said, "Dick, we've gotta do something about this."

I sent Dick the articles.

Dick got back with me and said, "Don't do anything, I'm on a plane. I'm coming back right now and we're gonna get on this."

Dick and I put our heads together and analyzed the story. We decided to demand that the CIA tell us the truth. We got a group of people together and went out to the gate of the CIA. We demanded to see the head of the CIA, even though we knew we weren't going to see him. The CIA arrested us.

Now, the funny thing about that is we had a group of people that went with us, and they were supposed to get arrested too. We're out with our picket signs and demonstration, and so the CIA apparently took a passive position.

They were probably thinking, "We're not gonna arrest them. They'll get tired and leave. It'll get dark, they'll leave."

But Dick and I had brought that yellow tape used on crime scenes with us. We wrapped the yellow tape around the gate of the CIA and then stood next to it and said, "This is a crime scene."

And they arrested our asses, probably thinking: "Oh, no, no. You're not going to do that." That was it.

Suddenly, folks are taking photographs and all that. Funny thing was everybody who was supposed to get arrested with us decided they weren't going to get arrested after all. So, the CIA took Dick and me off to Alexandria and booked us. At the same time we were in jail, there was this meeting at the Washington Convention Center. At the time, I think I was on WRC-AM, and Dick was doing something on WOL, so word got out that we had been arrested. And 5,000 people in that convention were ready to march on the jail where we were, so they let us out.

We kept making our demands to the CIA, and we even got Rep. Maxine Waters of California involved. Now, here's where I show you how talk radio works. I stayed on the air every day for four hours, I bet you, well over 90 days talking about this issue, demanding that the director of the CIA explain, even to the point that Larry King moderated a debate at the Palm Restaurant between Oliver North and me. And I had people from Costa Rica actually send me the indictment papers against Oliver North. That debate went on and on and on. If you recall, for the first time in history the director of the CIA actually went to California and met with the community. So, it ended up with myself, Dick and Maxine Waters really pushing that whole issue by going back to the CIA again. We kept the pressure on, and the last time we were arrested, Dick and I took sacks of flour and dumped them in front of the gate of the CIA to symbolize cocaine. Those fools actually brought dogs out to sniff.

After that arrest, we had to appear before a federal judge. The first time we were arrested, they found us guilty of a misdemeanor and we paid a fine and were released. The second time, though, the CIA wanted us arrested and kept in jail for 90 days. Then folks started saying they were going to surround the jail, so they cut a deal to get Dick and me out. The deal was that we would plead guilty — which we were — and we would not demonstrate in front of the CIA for a year. And if we agreed to that, the Feds would let us go.

You know, Black talk radio kept Gary Webb's story alive. Now, what we did never appeared in the movie, because if you saw *Kill the Messenger,* the 2014 film that starred Jeremy Renner as Webb, everything was based on the West Coast. Dick saw the movie and said the problem was that Gary Webb really didn't know what was going on back East. Gary was just focused on his problems on the West Coast because that's where his whole focus was. But he didn't connect our demonstrations here with the CIA. He does mention us in his book, but it was sort of like, "I was doing my thing and they were doing their thing."

We were out here on the East Coast, trying to get publicity, trying to get exposure, doing voter registration, knocking on doors. And then Jesse Jackson swoops in to get all the credit.

Not getting recognition for your work is part of the game. You come to grips with it. I would be dishonest if I say it didn't bother me. Of course, it bothers you. You're working hard, but the purpose is not personal recognition. By getting exposure, you allow your movement to grow.

You saw that in the movie *Selma.* The scene where the Student Nonviolent Coordinating Committee had been working in Selma for months before King arrived? When King got there, he came with cameras, news people and national attention. So, there was an automatic tension. Here we've been working on the ground. Then your leader comes in and gets all the attention. That comes with the territory.

But the bottom line is you don't stop because you just have to deal with it. Even to this day, you know, a Black leader like Rev. Al Sharpton gets attention whenever he shows up and gets involved, but he nurtured it. It's not something that he got automatically. He's been building it up for decades.

Sometimes stuff like the Gary Webb affair or the gangsta rap campaign can get you frustrated. You get angry. You appreciate small victories. You lose friends. People stop speaking to you.

But it's just the give and take of a movement. As former Rep. William Clay used to say, in politics there are no permanent friends or permanent enemies, only permanent interests.

CHAPTER 5

RUNNING TO LEAD THE NAACP

In the spring of 1993, the battle for who would replace Ben Hooks as head of the NAACP was heating up in Baltimore.

Benjamin Chavis, the civil rights veteran from North Carolina, was running for the executive director position, being backed by NAACP board chairman Dr. William Gibson, who was from South Carolina. But Chavis had that celebrity status from being part of the Wilmington Ten civil rights case, so this cabal, this group on the board, was trying to get the votes to have him elected executive director. The chair had a lot of influence on the board.

There were others running for the position: Earl Shinhoster, who ran the NAACP's Southeast region, Rev. Jesse Jackson and myself. And Jesse was really pushing and lobbying hard. He was funny. They thought he was an insider because he was from South Carolina too, like Gibson. He really wasn't. There was no way the board of the NAACP would ever allow Jesse to run the NAACP. Ever.

Chavis had an edge by virtue of having the Wilmington Ten reputation and the support of Gibson and other Carolina board members. Jesse ultimately dropped out and Chavis won.

But Chavis didn't have unanimous support. And the little-known relationship between Chavis and Nation of Islam Minister Louis

Farrakhan came as a total surprise to many board members. Chavis had close ties with the Nation of Islam and had grown close to its leader, Farrakhan. In fact, Chavis would later change his name to Minister Benjamin F. Muhammad and take over the Nation of Islam's most famous East Coast ministry: Muhammad's Mosque No. 7 in Harlem. Most NAACP board members were not going to allow this close connection to exist because of several prominent Jewish leaders on the board, like Rabbi David Saperstein. They were the first to raise hell when they learned that Chavis had developed a relationship with Farrakhan.

And Chavis didn't have much board support on this issue. Most people don't understand that the NAACP board can be conservative. These are older African Americans and some are corporate people, ministers and heads of fraternities and sororities.

But even if you didn't have the Jewish influence on the board, you also had major donors like the Ford Foundation and corporate America that the NAACP depended on.

During Chavis and Gibson's leadership, the NAACP Image Awards were in severe debt. It got so ridiculous that Gibson, the chairman of the board, and Chavis had private car service during that whole week in Hollywood. We are trying to get contributions from different organizations and the chairman of the board drives up to the Sony headquarters in a white stretch limousine. He is the one asking for contributions, but he rolls up in a stretch limo.

Well, the next year, we got rid of all the stretch limousines and got SUVs instead. That is how we controlled our expenses. When you were a cash cow, there is no real control over expenditures.

Let me give you another example. The chairman of the board bought a briefcase that cost over $600 and charged it to the NAACP. Actually, "60 Minutes" found out about it before we did. We went to the company he bought it from and asked, "What was the damn thing made of?" We were told it was made of ostrich skin.

"Well," we asked, "who buys that kind of thing?"

They said, and I will never forget this, "Someone who's trying to show off. Somebody that's trying to make an impression."

I suspect, although I don't know this for certain, that there was also a reduction in membership and contributions during this time period. So, in essence, the staff just wasn't doing its job. NAACP membership was down, grants were down, contributions were down, and expenses were up.

Another example: Chavis had leased two Lincoln sedans. We had a board meeting where we were trying to get control of the expenses. We were going over expenses with the audit committee, item by item — a long, tedious process.

Then, we got to a point where somebody asked, "What is this expense of two Lincolns?"

Chavis said, "I'm not certain, the contracts are upstairs in my office."

"Well, go up and get them. We'll wait." By then, there was little trust in Chavis, as the spending was clearly out of control.

It had gotten so bad that we ended up having to ask all the branches to empty their treasuries and send us money in order for the national office to stay open. And we asked for people to up their contributions. Organizations, institutions, corporations and individuals did just that, they came through for us. All I know is that we really played hardball with the expenses back then, and it really wasn't that difficult because once the forensic audit came in the board realized how much waste had taken place. The board was very appreciative of the fact that we were able to get expenses under control.

Membership in the NAACP wasn't declining because Blacks were making progress. No. Membership was declining because we were not actively seeking new memberships or renewals. We didn't have a good program.

Even though Bill Clinton had been elected president, we still had some major issues to tackle, like the apology for slavery. Remember, Clinton was not a big fan of welfare, but the NAACP had the whole welfare issue going on. We had affirmative action issues, we had reparation issues, we had voting registration issues, we had housing issues. I think these were self-inflicted wounds, that is the best way I can put it. We just were not well organized. Then you have to take into account the leadership at that time was simply not quality leadership.

NAACP IMAGE AWARDS

It all turned around when Myrlie Evers-Williams was elected chair of the National Board of Directors of the NAACP in 1995. When she became chair, the branches and the volunteers had renewed faith in the organization. She restructured the board and we started membership organizations. Myrlie asked me what committee I wanted to work on because I had helped to get her elected, and I had encouraged her to run. That is when I was asked to take over the Image Awards.

I had asked her for the Image Awards because, first off, nobody else wanted it. They knew the debt we were in.

I said, "You know what, give me the Image Awards. I think I can turn it around."

I had experience working as an executive director of the Detroit NAACP, which had its own money problems before I stepped in, so I thought I could use that experience to help with this project.

She said, "It's yours. Go for it."

The board agreed: "No problem. You can have that. Oh, yeah. You can have that."

Nobody else wanted it.

When I got the chairmanship of the NAACP Image Awards, I insisted that our treasurer, Charles Whitehead from Cincinnati, be the co-chair. His responsibility was to handle all the money, look over all the contracts and sign off on all expenditures. He worked for Procter & Gamble and he was a financial genius.

First, we did a forensic audit, and in doing so we identified where the waste was coming from in terms of the NAACP Image Awards. The awards ceremony was still in Los Angeles at this time. So we got rid of all the limousines, and then we got rid of all the hotel suites.

That was one process. We also were losing money by giving away Image Awards tickets to celebrities. That was the other process we needed to change. For instance, Little Richard wanted 20-something tickets. No matter who the celebrity was, he seemed to want 15 or more tickets. The tickets were the way we raised funds. So we're sitting there giving away half of the damn tickets to anybody who called themselves a celebrity. Even Rosa Parks, whom we honored at one event, wanted an extraordinary amount for all of her family and herself. And the most difficult thing I had to do was say no to Rosa Parks, especially after all we'd been through together. So, we were getting control of the finances and really just saying no to all these giveaways.

The other thing we did was product placement. People were placing their products at the Image Awards, but this time around we charged them. I went Hollywood on them: If you want your product to be featured, then you're going have to pay. That's how we ended up; we just cut our losses. We also suspended the Image Awards for one year so that we could regroup, get our expenses under control and bring in more revenue. At one point, people had thought about just eliminating the ceremony, because we were so in debt. They thought it was the end of the Image Awards. But we came back the next year.

Our other problem was that the Image Awards had the reputation of going all night long. The joke was to bring your lunch, dinner and breakfast. And we had too many categories. We had to curtail the categories and change the producer. Since we had the same producer for years, no one had really bothered to check how he was spending the money, so he was draining us with expenses. All we were doing was just writing checks.

I'll give you another example. One of the things we did was fire the African American accounting firm that counted the ballots. We went in and asked to meet with them at their office to see what kind of operation they had. They kept putting us off. We found out their office was their garage. And they were charging us a fortune.

To avoid any repercussions from firing an African American firm, we went out and hired the top white accounting firm and the top Black accounting firm. They agreed to do it as a team. Still, when we got rid of the other firm that was screwing us around, they raised holy hell.

"Oh, you're getting rid of us for a white firm?"

"No," we responded. "We got a Black firm. And we got a white firm. We got two of the top accounting firms in the country."

That is how we got around that issue. We saved a lot of money as well because the two firms didn't charge us in exchange for promotion. So, when it came time for the accounting firm to walk out on stage during the Image Awards, like they do at the Oscars, a Black representative walked out representing the Black firm, and a white guy walked out representing the other firm. That was in the true spirit of the NAACP.

THE CAMPAIGN AGAINST GANGSTER RAP

Every year, famed civil rights activist C. Delores Tucker had a luncheon of her national political women's organization, the National Congress of Black Women. At one of these luncheons, in the early nineties, R&B recording artists Dionne Warwick and Melba Moore showed up raising holy hell about the fact that the record industry was changing. They got wind of it because their sons, who were rappers, were trying to get recording contracts and were told that their music wasn't nasty enough. It wasn't gangster enough.

"I'm not here to sing. We got a problem," Warwick said to the group. "The music is changing, the message is changing and they got something called gangster rap now. And the lyrics you folks won't believe. Well, I'm here to ask y'all to help and that the women need to help. You're being called bitches, you're being called hos, and this has got to stop."

So, C. Delores answered the call. The next thing I know I get a call from her to come to her office on Christmas Eve with Dick Gregory.

"You guys have got to help me," she said. Then she started explaining what she wanted to do. We then hatched a plan to not go after the artist, but instead go after the record companies.

Oh, not just companies like Interscope Records. We went after its owner, Seagram. It was like the parent companies were the ones that were hiding their hand. Seagram owned all of Interscope, home to artists like Tupac Shakur, Eminem, Dr. Dre and Eve.

We went after the money behind the money. An artist might join a label, but didn't have any control. The parent company did.

And so C. Delores decided on our approach: Dick and I would demonstrate in front of record stores asking that the music have a rating system similar to that used for films, with labels like R, PG, G, etc. The other strategy was that she, nearly 70, and her husband would buy stock in the companies, then go to the stockholders' meeting and expose the music and the language to the stockholders. That image of a little old Black lady raising hell in the middle of a shareholders' meeting was priceless. And that's how the campaign got started, with C. Delores Tucker, Dick Gregory, Melba Moore and myself.

Of course, there was opposition. There's always going to be opposition. The rappers went after us — among them, Luther Campbell of 2 Live Crew and Suge Knight of Death Row Records. They denounced us and said we didn't understand the music. It was a battle.

But our issue was that this music was primarily directed at the Black community — at young, Black people — but much of it was bought by whites, and whites were making most of the profits. And we kept saying to them that you don't have white groups calling their women hos and bitches and doing this gangster rap. They're imitating us — and, in turn, disrespecting us. You don't have white guys out there doing that to their people.

White kids were the ones buying gangsta rap, but they weren't saying the same things about their own women. That was the bullshit behind it. They were emulating us, but the companies weren't insisting that the white gangster rap groups go out there calling somebody a ho or a nigga.

There was a double standard, and the double standard had to stop because it was detrimental to the community. And we had a long, drawn-out battle. There was even a Senate hearing on the issue. And what kind of impact was it having on the culture of the community?

Let me tell you what was interesting. We had a meeting with representatives of the record companies and C. Delores Tucker; Ofield Dukes, who was president of her organization; someone from the Bethune-DuBois Institute; and myself.

One of the first things the representatives from the record companies asked us was, "What do you want?"

And I'm thinking, "What do you mean, what do we want? We want you to do A, B and C. We want these records, these CDs labeled. We want this gangster rap to stop, you know? We want radio stations to give other music an opportunity to be heard."

But that's not what they meant.

They meant, "What do you want? How much? What will it take to…?"

They thought we were there for a shakedown.

And to a person, all of us on the other side responded, "You've got the wrong group of people. Not one of us is here for a shakedown. We don't want a damn thing. You don't have enough to buy us off."

I never will forget that. It wasn't that we had communicated with each other, or that we had planned what we would say.

But, we all independently said, "Well, no, I don't want anything from you. I don't want anything. I'll tell you what I want — I want this shit to stop."

And that was very strange to the record companies. They came, you know, bearing gifts. So there was no quid pro quo. None.

THE RADIO ONE YEARS

My station got sold.

WWRC was initially in Washington, a powerhouse owned by NBC. Then, during the whole media thing with President Clinton's Telecommunications Act of 1996, some owners had to sell off properties in order to conform to the new law limiting multiple ownership of stations. So WWRC ended up being bought by another company and then was sold several more times.

After WWRC was sold, Cathy Hughes asked me if I would join WOL — do a talk show and become program director. She couldn't afford or wasn't willing to pay my salary strictly as a talk show personality, so she doubled up my duties. Initially, we did it out of Baltimore, because it was WOL-AM and WOLB, and she had just bought some stations. In fact, her company, Radio One, started buying a lot of stations. So, I would commute to work, then do my show before serving as program director.

My show was not in the same time slot — now midday. Doing the radio show was not a problem. The biggest challenge was being a program director. I will never, ever, ever be a program director again. You would have to pay me a fortune. And being on the air was very difficult because there was no time to prep.

It takes a lot to prep for a show. A lot of people think you just come in, do four hours and you leave. And that's the end of your day. The reality is it takes hours to prep — to read the newspapers, research, watch old tapes, listen to other stations. In news talk radio, you're always prepping since news is always happening.

I still did news talk at this station because in talk radio you've got to be true to yourself. You can't be phony. If you're conservative, you've got to be conservative. If you're a liberal, you've got to be a liberal. You've got to be what you are because the voice doesn't lie. People can pick you out if you're not who you really are.

So, as a program director, my biggest problem was trying to manage other personalities. For example, there was a brother named C. Miles Smith. C. Miles was a star. I mean, C. Miles was a natural in talk radio. He was a Morehouse man from Atlanta. We had heavy hitters like him. We had C. Miles, Bernie McCain, and there was former state senator

Clarence Mitchell III's daughter, journalist Lisa Mitchell. I also brought aboard another former state senator whom Mrs. Hughes wanted on the air, Larry Young. Larry is still on the air at WOLB doing mornings. He was rather controversial and had gotten into some alleged legal trouble, but he was well-respected and well-known in Baltimore. Then there was a sports guy named Butch McAdams. All of them were relatively good folks.

Once I tried to give Lisa Mitchell a prime-time spot — morning drive. Man, she got pissed at me. She did not want to do morning talk. And I didn't understand at the time, but it was primarily because she had to take her children to school in the morning. I guess it was too difficult for her, but since I was the program director, I had to put people where I thought they were supposed to be. But anytime you made a move, the one thing that people would always say was, "I'm gonna tell Mrs. Hughes."

You really couldn't make a decision until she approved it. But it's funny. People in Baltimore are a different animal, different audience, a different group of people. They're not Washingtonians. Folk in Baltimore don't like Washingtonians and Washingtonians don't like folk in Baltimore. It has just always been like that. So, here we are trying to balance between two competing cities. Baltimore is a blue-collar town, where folks work in the plants and generations of families often live in the same neighborhoods they were born in. Washington is a white-collar town, home to more professionals and government employees. So, we had different audiences that made it interesting. Eventually, we moved to Washington, and the two stations finally separated. But that, of course, was a temporary fix.

Now there was some controversy about putting Larry on air, but Larry Young turned out to be a first-class talk show personality. As a matter of fact, he's listed in *Talkers Magazine* among the top 100 radio show hosts, and he is still on the air after more than 20 years. But then there was C. Miles Smith. C. Miles was a character, man.

C. Miles made his reputation in Atlanta. He used to call into a right-wing station, on WSB, one of the Cox stations that used to feature Herman Cain. C. Miles was a caller that the conservatives loved to talk to because he was critical of Black leadership, so he sort of became a personality. They soon gave him a job.

Well, the show was quirky. C. Miles was kind of quirky. He was a drama major from Morehouse. Apparently, he was in the same class as Samuel L. Jackson. C. Miles understood the theater of the mind. He was at WOL-Baltimore before I got there, but man, he was the most difficult dude in the world to manage. You couldn't do anything to please him, but people loved him. He had character, but he went after elected officials. There's a word for it: irreverent.

C. Miles also had this bad habit of talking about other talk personalities that he didn't like, both on the job and on air. This is a no-no in the business, especially those that are on your station. C. Miles also had a habit of going after Black elected officials and Black leadership. That was his whole shtick. People loved him.

But then C. Miles got on the air one day and suggested that the mayor of Baltimore, Kurt Schmoke, was defending the police chief because the police chief might have had compromising photos of the mayor in some illicit sexual situation. Well, man, Mayor Schmoke picks up the phone and calls Cathy's son, Alfred Liggins, whom he knows. Then, Alfred calls me into his office, since I'm the program director, and says, "What are we going to do about this? The mayor is threatening to sue me, and sue the station. We're gonna have to suspend him. Obviously."

So we suspended C. Miles.

Of course, C. Miles was terribly upset, as you can imagine. Nobody likes to be suspended. I had been suspended once by a program director in Detroit because I was talking about religion and some of the myths of religion. Well, apparently somewhere between suspending C. Miles and C. Miles coming back, Alfred just fired him. So before he got off the air, C. Miles started referring to Cathy Hughes — the founder — as a bitch. And then he was gone. C. Miles caused his own demise because you just can't defame people like that without any proof.

Funny thing is he wasn't conservative. He was the militant voice on the show. He started off being the favorite of white right-wing personalities in Atlanta, like he was their fair-haired boy. They loved him because he talked about Hosea Williams and the NAACP, and he hated Andrew Young. So, anything the right-wingers said, he seconded. That's why they loved him and gave him a show. Then he comes to Baltimore and becomes this militant host. He is still talking about Black leadership, but here's the difference: He's talking about Black leadership to Black people. So, you know, folk kind of fell into it.

They would say, "Yeah, you're right, brother. They can't relate to us."

So, there is a difference when you're on Black talk shows, talking about Black folk. But he really didn't have a right-wing agenda. His niche was that Black leadership was out of touch. That's what it was. Out of touch. When he was talking to white people in Atlanta it was about incompetence. Then C. Miles ended up back in Atlanta, not working, had a brain aneurysm and almost died.

Here's the other part of my Radio One story. It became apparent that it was too difficult for me to be a personality on air and a program director. It was just too much. And my daughter Shawna was my assistant because she had been with me at WWRC. So, when I came over to WOL, I brought her with me as my assistant program director because she had always wanted to get into radio. Of course, she ended up getting her own morning show on the FM station in Baltimore. And there's a story there too because she got fired. But let's go back to my story.

Cathy Hughes said to me, "Well, we've realized we can't do that anymore. It's just too difficult."

A lot of Black stations gave you two jobs in order to afford personalities.

She said, "It's just not gonna work."

Now the problem was that she wanted to cut my salary by 70 percent. Man, you could've heard me in Connecticut.

The vice president calls me in and says, "Oh, we've gotta cut your salary."

I mean, it was like going from $70,000 down to $30,000. I wouldn't have been able to afford to live.

So I said, "Oh no!" I just wouldn't accept it.

"Joe, if I pay you this amount, this throws my payroll out of whack," Cathy said. "I've got to pay you, and I've got all these stations in other cities."

Of course, I didn't give a damn. I've got to live. Finally, they gave in to my demand and I got paid. And then Shawna goes on to be a co-host on a really popular FM station in Baltimore owned by Radio One. We both worked for Radio One at the same time. That is how I stayed at WOL.

Now here is my biggest criticism of many Black radio stations: Many of them are programmed by white people. People don't know this. For example, the music stations at Radio One in Baltimore had a white music program director. He was a nice guy who knew his job and all that, but then one day John F. Kennedy Jr. died in an airplane crash, and they had to address that.

But the thing was, the day before the plane crash, a popular Black pastor in Baltimore was killed in his driveway while taking groceries out of the trunk of his car. People were devastated, and listeners were calling the show crying and sharing stories about the many ways he had helped the community.

Then JFK Jr. died the next day, and Shawna was told to dedicate the show to him. Some people called in about that, but not as many as the day before. One of the callers mentioned that the Kennedy family made its fortune from illegal activities. Shawna knew about the rumored Kennedy family bootleg empire but all she knew about JFK Jr. was his work as editor of *George* magazine and his reputation as a playboy. She said, "Exactly, and all we really hear about JFK Jr. is he has a magazine and he dated Madonna. We've got bigger problems in our community. I mean, I care but at the same time I don't."

The program director quickly called Shawna into his office to lecture her about the importance of the Kennedy family in Maryland. Kathleen Kennedy Townsend, Robert Kennedy's daughter, was lieutenant governor of Maryland at the time. And the program director was from Boston, so he backed the whole Kennedy phenomenon that believed, "Oh, you just don't say anything like that."

Shawna said, "Well, it's true. In the Black community he had the reputation of being a playboy."

For her comments, Shawna was suspended for one week. When she returned, she was informed that her contract would not be renewed, and that was her last day on the air.

Cathy Hughes didn't say anything — just let her get fired. I went to Cathy and said, "This is wrong," but she wouldn't override her program director.

Here's the problem that WOL had: It was only a 1,000-watt station. Cathy Hughes was the owner of WOL, but *she* was the personality as well. She put WOL on the map.

And in 1986 she had what was called the "Take It Back" protest, where people would go down to the *Washington Post* office and throw back their newspapers in protest of the negative depiction of the Black community in the first issue of the newly redesigned Sunday magazine. The cover story featured a photo of Just-Ice, a rapper from New York who was accused of a murder in Washington, and the magazine included a "Critic at Large" column by a writer who was sympathetic to store owners who refused to admit young Black men for fear of shoplifting.

Well, thousands of listeners all day on Sunday would drive by and throw their *Washington Posts* out of the car before and after church. Katharine Graham, the publisher, and her son Donald came to work one Monday morning and saw thousands of their newspapers blowing in the street, so she gets on the phone with Cathy and the rest is history. Three weeks before Christmas, advertisers pulled out of the magazine and the *Post* eventually compromised.

Again, this story shows the true tradition of Black talk radio as an activist instrument. And it was such a smart move because she didn't say boycott the newspaper, and she didn't say read it. She just said when you get through with it, or if you don't read it, throw it back. Well, who was impacted by that throwback? The advertisers suffer, especially on Sundays because the coupon section is the biggest edition of the week.

SATELLITE RADIO WAS MADE FOR ME

Before there was SiriusXM, there was Sirius Satellite Radio and there was XM Satellite Radio.

XM Satellite Radio, the larger of the two satellite radio companies at the time and based in Washington, D.C., had developed a partnership with Radio One to provide content for five channels, and General Motors was a major partner and investor in XM. So they had what they call these third-party relationships. Four of the channels were music — spiritual and rap. One of the channels was talk — specifically Black talk. And I had suggested that we call it "The Power" because the slogan at WOL was "Information is Power."

Alfred Liggins is a smart businessperson, and his mother Cathy Hughes is a smart businessperson, so they saw an opportunity to get onboard with satellite radio. The irony is, they hated it. But all terrestrial radio owners hated satellite radio at the time. They thought: 1) it wasn't going to last because no one was going to pay for radio, and 2) it could very well be the demise of terrestrial radio. And this term terrestrial radio is something they had never used before. It came about because of satellite radio. Before, it was just called *radio*. So what's terrestrial?

Terrestrial means land. In other words, it means antenna versus satellite. Oh man, owners of terrestrial radio stations had the same reaction as people comparing regular TV to satellite TV. And they were like AM radio owners who hated when FM came onboard.

Today, who listens to AM? Young people can't stand AM, except if it's sports. My children get in the car and I might turn to an AM station and they go, "What is that?" Their ears can't even handle it.

Sirius, the smaller of the two satellite radio companies, was headquartered in New York. In essence, Radio One provided XM with content — they just took our shows and our formats and took them virtually straight to air. Problem was that satellite radio did not have the same restrictions that terrestrial radio had from the FCC. Unlike terrestrial radio, on satellite you could curse, talk about sex and use all seven of George Carlin's "seven dirty words."

That's why Howard Stern left FM radio in New York to go over to satellite. (Well, that and a boatload of money.) He could say anything he wanted to say. Satellite was made for Howard Stern. And satellite radio was made for me.

There was a little Jewish lady named Lynn Samuels. She used to be on WABC in New York, doing fill-in work. She was the stereotypical, straight, West Side, little Jewish lady. You can visualize her with a bun in the back of her head, but man, she could drop the "F" bomb a thousand times an hour. And she could do that on satellite radio. So, here I was caught between Radio One and the rules of terrestrial radio, and satellite radio, the XM people and the wild, wild West.

The satellite people would say, "We don't want you guys (the programmers) to sound like terrestrial radio."

"My God," we would say, "but we are."

"Ah well."

If I dared to say a curse word when Radio One's WOL was on with XM, the first people I'd hear from would be WOL listeners who would pick up the phone.

"I'm gonna tell Mrs. Hughes. You cursed on the air. You said damn."

But then the folks over at XM said, "Yeah, that's what we want to hear!"

So a breakup was inevitable. The split happened when XM decided it was not going to accept ads because it was going to be commercial-free, but this applied only to its music channels. And XM enacted this policy without informing its third-party partners.

So Alfred made a business decision. It didn't make financial sense for Radio One to stay on satellite radio. He pulled all the music channels, which forced XM to create in-house stations or channels for music — two hip-hop channels. But they kept the talk channels because XM could sell ads on the talk format. Unfortunately, Radio One didn't know how to capitalize on that. In addition, you had the schizophrenia going on.

"I don't like satellite radio," they'd say. "I don't trust satellite radio."

It was weird.

So I was caught in between serving two masters. At this time, the President of the United States (POTUS) channel was being developed on XM. Nate Davis was president of XM then. He was a smooth brother who was smart and bright. Anyway, I had been invited to go to a reception for the launching of POTUS, and he came up to me. There had been a rumor floating around that they were going to offer me a contract. They wanted me in-house because Radio One and XM were going to split and withdraw the talk channel.

I will never forget that I was with my wife, Sherry, when Nate came by and said, "Look, I know you're hearing a lot of rumors, but I'm here to tell you I don't know what's going to happen between Radio One and XM. But nothing's going to happen with you. We want you. We want *you* and we will do whatever it takes to get you on XM, to keep you on XM."

And I said, "Oh, OK."

A few weeks or a couple months later, man, they made me an offer to come in-house and join XM.

So I, in essence, left Radio One and was fully employed. The initial contract was that Radio One paid part of my salary and XM paid part of my salary. This allowed Cathy Hughes to pay me what I was worth, at least in part. But Radio One still wanted to carry my morning show. So, they worked out an agreement where XM would pay Radio One to carry my show and that would come to me in my contract. But XM really didn't like it.

"Why would people who can hear you free then take a subscription?" they asked. "But let's go ahead and do it because there's what's called a legacy. You're a legacy and it might help with people who want to hear you clearer. Because they can't hear you once they go under a bridge, or in a building. And if they leave town, they can't hear it. Plus, there's a whole country out here that should hear you, so if you want …"

I said, "You know what? I'm still loyal to Radio One. Let's just stay."

We made this financial agreement, but it was just for a fraction of the money, and that went on for a while.

Then, in 2008, Sirius and XM merged and Mel Karmazin came on to take over the combined company. He was the CEO at Sirius before the merger. It was interesting when that merger took place. So, I'm doing my radio show over at the XM building when Mel walks into the studio and introduces himself.

I said, "Well, would you be willing to come on the air and explain this merger? Because people don't know the merger."

And he said, "I'll come on your show any day."

As a matter of fact, I was the only show he ever came on. Mel came, sat down, then explained to Black people what the merger meant. He and I became very close. When the time came to renew my contract, we still had this split with the funds. My agent says to Alfred, "Wait a minute, you guys are only paying him $10,000." And I never will forget what my agent said to Alfred:

"Alfred, I don't know, but in case you haven't gotten the word, slavery has been over 100 years." But they didn't increase it.

And I told my agent, "Look, don't sweat it."

Mel came to me and put me on a whole different level.

"If I were you, I wouldn't waste time with them," he said. "What they're offering you, I spend on lunches, but it's up to you. I don't even want their money. It's yours. I'll just give it to you. If I were you, I wouldn't even negotiate with them because if you've got to start that low you don't even need to bother. Matter of fact, we'll double your salary, so you don't have to worry about it."

Quite candidly, XM didn't want me on terrestrial radio, but I went ahead and stayed with Radio One awhile. Now by the time the next contract comes up, this would have been the second or third contract renewal every two years, and we were a household name. We were national and well-established. In fact, I was like No. 10 on the best talk show list.

Finally, my agent said, "Look, you can't do this any longer. This does not make sense." Alfred didn't even have the decency to return my agent's call, and he didn't call me. This used to upset me because when Alfred needed someone to go to the city council to argue a position on behalf of Radio One, he would always call me. I'd show up for him.

I never said no. That's why it really bothered me when Alfred didn't call.

When Radio One decided to syndicate its talk program, they brought in Michael Eric Dyson and Al Sharpton, but they never offered me an opportunity to be syndicated on Radio One. Now stop and think about this: I'm doing a national show on XM and then you bring on two people, particularly Michael Eric Dyson, and you give him a syndicated show. But that didn't work well. I think Sharpton was a natural, and Michael Eric was very good too. Both of them were very good, had great content, and knew what they were talking about, but I'm just sitting up here saying, "Why are you dissing me?" It doesn't make sense.

Well, Alfred's argument was that it was a business decision. Radio One didn't want to take me off mornings, but they wanted the stations they had bought in other cities, like Richmond, to have local programming because there was this concern that too much of the programming was national and people were losing local content.

So here I was doing the morning show, and they weren't prepared to syndicate their morning AM talk. Then we found out that they were streaming my show and weren't telling us. So, we gave them a few months during the contract negotiations to make an offer, but Alfred never made an offer, never returned a phone call and never spoke about it. So, now it was time for *me* to make a business decision.

So, I left Radio One and joined XM.

Truth be told, Cathy and Alfred were not the biggest fans of satellite radio anyway. But they also knew the numbers behind AM talk were not what they used to be.

AM radio was no longer the cash cow. You could triple the ratings on AM — like I did at WOL — and still didn't bring in as much revenue as your FM station. So even though WOL was the first radio station Cathy Hughes owned, and it was her baby, she now had expanded to FM stations — not only in Washington, D.C, but across the country.

FM stations were cash cows supported by ads. Much of AM, however, is a loss leader. Plus, news talk — especially if it wasn't from a conservative perspective — was becoming less in demand. Advertisers didn't want the Bob Laws, the Gary Byrds, and the Joe Madisons on the air because that political atmosphere had changed. Our shows were counter to the political pendulum that was swinging to the right.

And if the Black owners wanted to remain relevant or remain in business, they had to more and more focus on the bottom line. And that game is advertising. Plus, you're under added pressure because, with the Telecommunication Act of 1996, companies like Clear Channel or Cumulus could own four or five stations. You had to compete or die.

So that meant you could own a sports talk station, a talk station, or even two talk stations. You could own both a music station and a rock station. But they had to bring in advertising — and revenue.

I always make a habit of visiting radio stations and going on the air when I give speeches. I once went to Fort Wayne, Indiana, and asked, "Do you guys have a Black station here?"

They had one station, which was a sunset station. What's a sunset station? A sunset station goes off the air at sundown, then primarily plays religious music — or maybe a public affairs show — on weekends. The only other game in town was this one company that owned all the other radio stations. So, that meant you could bundle the advertising. This means if I owned many stations, I could go to a car dealer or a prospective advertiser and say, "Look, for X amount of money I can get you on the sports station and on the music station. I can get you on three stations, four stations."

Of course, this makes it extremely difficult for a sole owner like Radio One to compete.

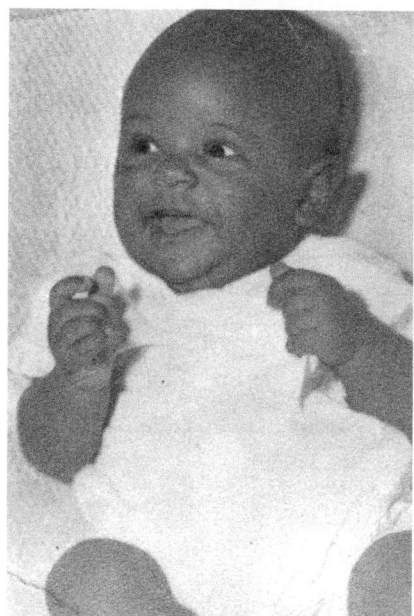

Joe Madison as a toddler, with his little sister, Yvonne, his grandfather, Jim Stone, and his mother, Nancy Stone. Bottom: Joe as an infant, and in his yearbook photo from Roosevelt High School, 1967.

TOP AND BOTTOM LEFT: MADISON FAMILY; BOTTOM RIGHT: "FINDING YOUR ROOTS"

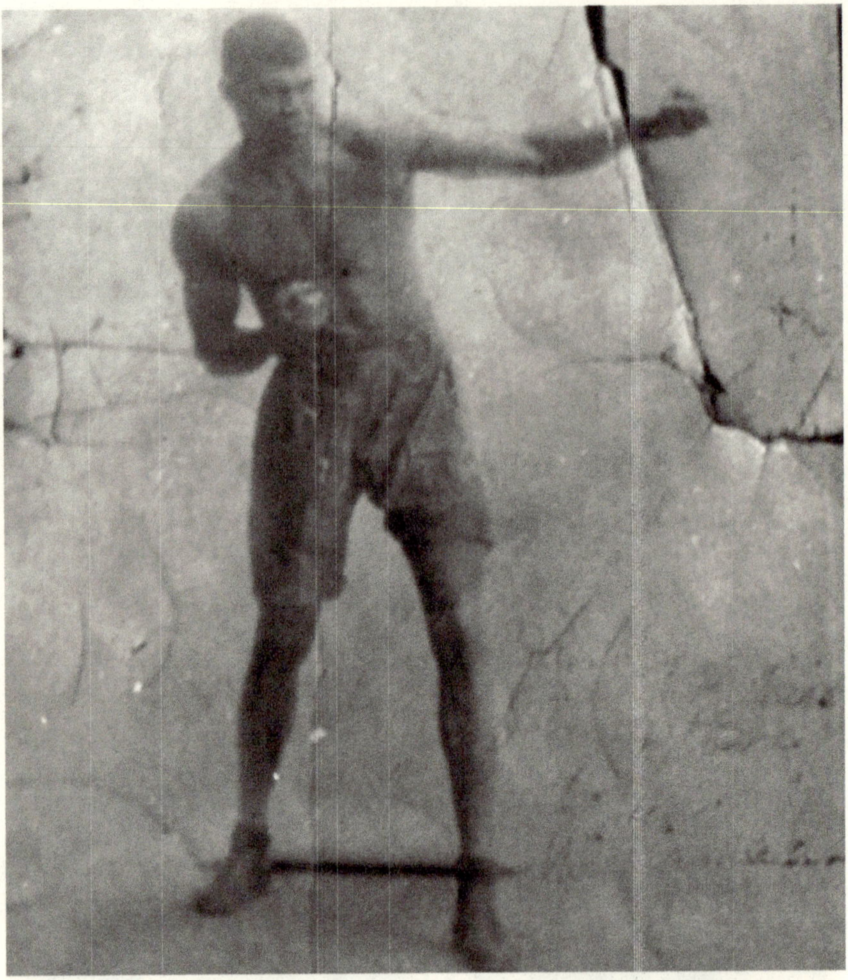

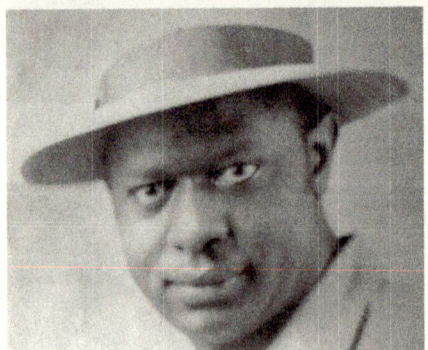

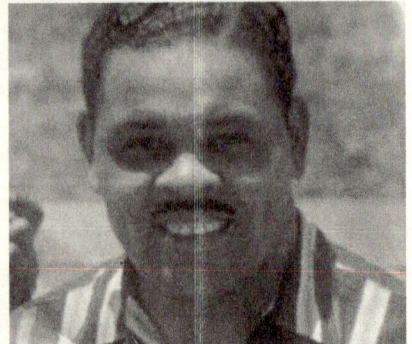

Top: Joe's grandfather, Jim Stone, was a professional boxer. Bottom left: Felix Madison, the man Joe knew as his father. Bottom right: Joe's biological father, Herman Haygood.

TOP AND BOTTOM LEFT: MADISON FAMILY; BOTTOM RIGHT: "FINDING YOUR ROOTS"

Joe Madison playing football for Washington University in St. Louis.

Top left: Joe poses for a photo that appeared with a 1970 profile of him in the Washington University magazine, "A Man for All Seasons." Top right: Joe sings with a Washington University choir at the Lincoln Center in New York. Bottom: Joe in his current SiriusXM radio studio in Washington.

TOP LEFT AND RIGHT: WASHINGTON UNIVERSITY PHOTOGRAPHIC SERVICES COLLECTION

Top: Joe receives an honorary doctorate from Washington University in 2019.
Bottom: Joe and Sharon Madison with Barack and Michelle Obama at a White House Correspondents Dinner.

Top: Joe poses with the Four Tops, showing off their identical "Black Eagle" watches. Bottom: With comedian George Wallace.

SHARON MADISON

Top: Joe with renowned civil rights activist Rosa Parks. Bottom: Joe and Sharon with Michelle Obama.

Top: With civil rights activist and former presidential candidate Jesse Jackson. Bottom: With the "Dream Team" of lawyers representing defendants accused of handcuffing themselves to the Sudan Embassy. In front, from left: attorney Kenneth Starr; defendants Walter Fauntroy, Joe Madison and Michael Horowitz; attorney Johnnie Cochran; and comedian Dick Gregory, who was charged in a separate case.

Top: With NAACP Chairman Julian Bond and comedian Dick Gregory. Bottom: With John Carlos, the American track star known for giving a Black Power salute on the medal stand at the 1968 Olympics in Mexico City.

Left: With Harvard Professor Henry Louis "Skip" Gates Jr. at a White House reception. Right: With CNN anchor Anderson Cooper in Haiti, covering the 2010 earthquake.

With Congressman Kweisi Mfume, then-Sen. Barack Obama and civil rights activist Al Sharpton, at the Save Darfur rally on Capitol Hill. After everyone autographed the photo, Obama laughed and complained that Mfume signed his name on top of Obama's face.

TOP LEFT AND RIGHT: SHARON MADISON

Top: With Eric Holder, attorney general under President Barack Obama, talking about redistricting plans. Bottom: With Gen. Colin Powell, secretary of state under President George W. Bush, at the South Sudan flag-raising ceremony.

SHARON MADISON

Distributing "sacks of hope" from Christian Solidarity International and meeting with villagers in South Sudan, including boys rescued from slavery.

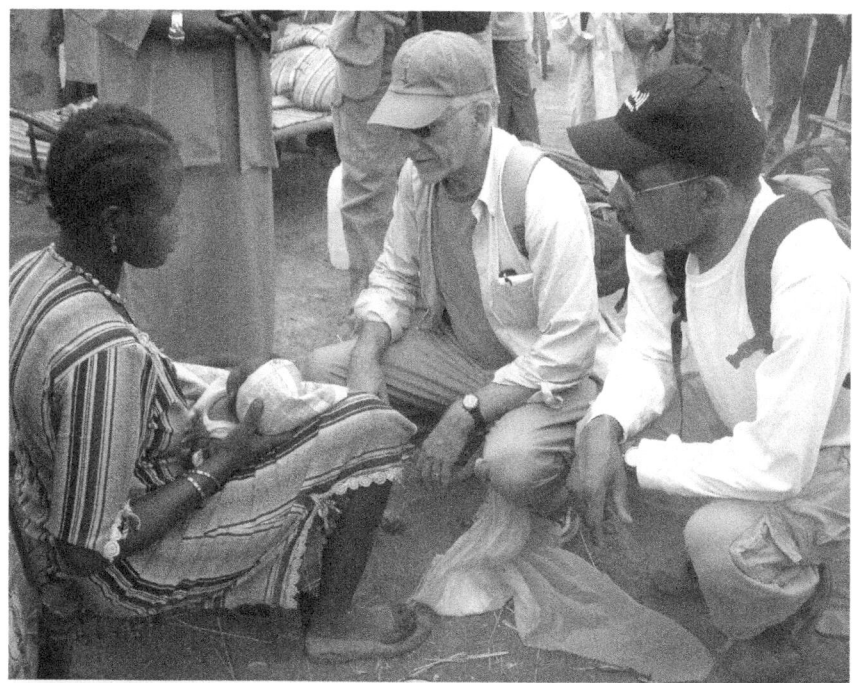

Top: Joe Madison and John Eibner of Christian Solidarity International talk to a Dinka woman with a baby who had been displaced from her home in South Sudan by war but was repatriated during the peace process. Bottom: Joe shakes hands with then-Sen. Joe Biden.

TOP: CHRISTIAN SOLIDARITY INTERNATIONAL

Top: Joe interviews President Barack Obama in the Oval Office in 2010.
Bottom: Joe poses with a plaque noting his induction into the Radio Hall of Fame in 2019.

TOP: PETE SOUZA, WHITE HOUSE; BOTTOM: SHARON MADISON

CHAPTER 6

THE SUDAN CAMPAIGN

The Sudan campaign started because a representative from Christian Solidarity International (CSI) in Zurich contacted me. At the time, John Garang was president of the Southern Sudan Autonomous Region — known today as South Sudan. The representative knew me from my radio show. He had been working in Sudan during its 22-year civil war, so he came to me because he wanted the support of the Congressional Black Caucus and African Americans. I suspect that by that time I had a reputation for doing these kinds of things.

So, he asked if I would be willing to go to Sudan to see what was happening with women and children being taken as slaves in the civil war. They would raid villages. The men would be killed, then they would take the women and children as bounty to be sold.

The representative said, "Look, it's a dangerous trip. They're in the middle of a civil war." He didn't sugarcoat it.

He said, "We can't tell people we're going. We go under the auspices of the South Sudanese government that they have established."

We literally had to fly zigzag over the country to keep from being shot down. Once I was there, I had the opportunity to witness the work of CSI as an organization that raised money all over the world to buy the freedom of slaves — mostly women and children. What they would do is raise money globally, then go into South Sudan and pretend to be slave traders. Instead, they would buy the freedom of women and children.

The first time I went I saw 800 South Sudanese people sitting under a tree. Their freedom had just been purchased. And there was a process where they were photographed so that if they were recaptured, they could be identified. Some people were very critical of this process because they didn't think you should buy people's freedom. My position was, hell, during American slavery we bought folks' freedom all the time.

Some organizations like UNICEF were part of the debate and would say things like: "Oh, how do you know what's happening?" and, "Are they using you guys?"

I thought, "Hey, we have to do whatever it takes to get these folks back home to their villages."

I had never seen anything like it. I saw a woman who had her breast burned off with a torch because she was nursing a baby. She had refused to stop, so the soldiers just burned her breast off. I met a 16-year-old girl who was taken as a slave, raped by her captives, then forced to have sex with her brother in front of them. This was horrendous stuff. I also saw a baby crawling around in a minefield, and then a guy who's now a politician literally walked through that minefield to pick up the baby.

I met two men whose wives were taken. They had tracked the kidnappers through the brush and attempted to free them. The men were caught and their arms were chopped off up to the elbow. So CSI bought them prostheses. Prior to that, these men couldn't even relieve themselves without their wives' help. They were useless in the village because men without hands couldn't build their huts or work the fields. They couldn't do anything. These two men have since died.

With temperatures reaching 110 degrees or more, we often had to go off to the side of the road to find shade, or we would be out in the bush in the hot sun. We'd seek refuge under massive mahogany trees, which ended up being the gathering place for many of the men in the village. But to talk with the women, sometimes, we had to peel away from the main body of villagers because if they heard the stories of the atrocities, a lot of times these women wouldn't be accepted back in the villages. One young lady who was pregnant gave birth to her child in a goat pen, then she had to run away. Part of the strategy of the rebels was to rape women and impregnate them as part of their war effort.

TAKING UP THE CAUSE

We interviewed these people in South Sudan and got their eyewitness testimony. My job was to get their stories, return to the United States and try to convince Congress to help them by passing the Sudan Peace Act.

One of the people who traveled and worked closely with us was Rep. Donald Payne of New Jersey. He was called "Mr. Africa." I worked with Donald to convince the Congressional Black Caucus to give Sudan aid. We even held a joint news conference with members of the Congressional Black Caucus and conservatives like Rep. Dick Armey of Texas.

Just before the news conference, Rep. Charles Rangel of New York came up to me and said, "In the 40 years that I've been in the United States Congress, I have never been on a stage with Dick Armey. You're the first person that has made that happen."

That is how some right-wing conservatives took up the Christian cause of this war in Sudan. Unfortunately, many Congressional Black Caucus members didn't know what was happening. It just wasn't on their radar. That is why I felt it was my responsibility to put this civil war on the radio.

And then we moved on to direct action.

We demonstrated in front of the Sudan Embassy almost on a weekly basis. We got arrested, sometimes, alongside members of Congress. Rep. John Lewis got arrested with us, as did Prof. Ron Walters. I never will forget that five grandmothers who called themselves "The Grandmothers" also got arrested.

At one point I got arrested for handcuffing myself to the front door of the Sudanese Embassy, along with former Congressman Walter Fauntroy of Washington, D.C., and a conservative activist named Michael Horowitz, of the Hudson Institute. We were arrested for trespassing and were taken to jail.

In the lockup, Horowitz started bragging about how he knew Kenneth Starr, who led the Monica Lewinsky investigation that got Bill Clinton impeached. And Horowitz said that when we went to court, he was going to get Ken Starr to represent him.

So as a kind of one-upmanship, I started bragging about how I knew Johnnie Cochran, who of course had been the lead defense attorney for O.J. Simpson, and I said I was going to get Johnnie Cochran to represent me.

Then I started thinking: Well, hell, why don't we see if both of them would agree to defend us. Talk about a "Dream Team." Michael Horowitz agreed and contacted Ken Starr, and Ken Starr said he would do it if Johnnie Cochran did. And I contacted Johnnie Cochran, and he said *he* would do it if Ken Starr did.

So when the court date came up, Johnnie Cochran flew in from L.A., and we met at Ken Starr's office at his law firm in D.C. The two lawyers greeted each other warmly, and then we all took a cab to the courthouse.

So as you can imagine, as we enter the courtroom, there was an immediate buzz, because in walks Johnnie Cochran and Kenneth Starr to represent these three Africa activists. And the funny thing was, the courtroom filled up immediately.

Starr and Cochran went back and forth about who was going to be the lead attorney. Johnnie told Ken, "This is your city, so you take the lead." But Ken told Johnnie, "No, no, this is your *country,* you're the celebrity, you take the lead."

When the judge came out, I started laughing, and I leaned over and told Horowitz, "We've got this made, because I've known the judge since she was a teacher." Her mother was an NAACP board member, and I had known the family for years.

Johnnie ended up taking the lead, and when the trial started, he stood up and said, "I'm Johnnie Cochran, counsel for Michael Horowitz, and Kenneth Starr, my co-counsel, is here to represent Joe Madison and Walter Fauntroy." They had somehow decided to swap defendants — the firebrand Black defense attorney representing the white conservative, and the conservative white constitutional expert representing the brash Black activists.

The judge actually turned to the prosecutor and asked, "Do you really want to go ahead with this case?" And the young federal prosecutor said, "Yes, we plan to go forward with the charges."

And they made their arguments that this was an act of civil disobedience, and it took no more than a half an hour, most of which was formalities. The thing is, we were pleading guilty, because we *were* guilty. That's what civil disobedience is all about — you break the law in order to get attention for the cause.

And so they found us guilty, and we were fined $50 and released.

That judge could have sentenced us to jail, but she just said, you guys are guilty, call it a day.

After the trial, we went outside and held a news conference. All the media was there to lay eyes on two of the most recognizable attorneys in the country. That gave us an opportunity to talk about the civil war in Sudan and the taking of slaves.

The funny thing was, the prosecutor came up to me with a big smile on his face, pulled me aside and said, "Mr. Madison, I'd like to talk to you for a moment." And he said, "I want to thank you very much because I can now go back to the office and say I just defeated Ken Starr and Johnnie Cochran in court." And he just skipped away.

Actors Danny Glover and Don Cheadle joined the cause. George Clooney got involved too, and we became friends. Then, the Darfur movement started and that brought us a lot of attention, but I had been in and out of South Sudan six or seven times before Clooney got there.

That's when I met then-Sen. Barack Obama. There is a great photo of Al Sharpton (who also went on several trips to Sudan), Sen. Obama, Rep. Kweisi Mfume and myself. It's a classic photograph. We're all at this Darfur rally, along with Clooney and former NBA star Manute Bol, trying to gain support for the refugees of Darfur.

There are reams of stories about Sudan and the Darfur movement. We also had a divestment strategy. We were very successful. As a matter of fact, one of the first persons to advocate for divestment was Maryland Lt. Gov. Michael Steele, a Republican.

My wife also went to Sudan with me. And let me pause to tell you something about my wife, Sherry. She was at my side during virtually every episode described in this book. We have been married since 1977, and this is a woman who went to Sudan with me — to a war zone! I couldn't get that little chump Armstrong Williams — conservative talk show host turned TV station owner — to go to a war zone with me. But my wife went.

When I went to Sudan one time, I said, "Armstrong, you got to come with me. Fauntroy has gone with me, so you've gotta come."

But you know what that little Negro Armstrong said to me?

"There's a war going on."

That is why he wouldn't go.

And Armstrong wasn't alone. When I first started going to Sudan and had just gotten back, I was attending a function around the time that Al Sharpton's National Action Network had just started, and Geraldo

Rivera was there. I had been interviewed by Geraldo years before, so I started talking to him about my trip.

I said, "Geraldo, you've got to come to Sudan."

He said, "Well, can I get there in a day and get back?"

"Man," I said, "this is South Sudan. No, you can't."

"Well, what hotel we gonna stay in, Joe?"

"Hotel? Motherfucker, we're gonna be sleeping in tents in the bush."

He wouldn't go either.

At the time, many Christian conservatives were at the heart of the relief efforts in Sudan, so it made sense to reach out to conservatives like Armstrong and Geraldo. But they weren't interested.

But there were four white folks who did go with me to Sudan: Rusty Humphries, a conservative; Thom Hartmann, an international relief worker and progressive broadcaster; Jack Rice, a former CIA officer turned media analyst; and Ellen Ratner, whose brother used to own the Brooklyn Nets basketball team.

So this is why I have more respect for my wife, who went with me, even though she didn't have to go. After my first trip, she saw the impact that Sudan had on me, but she didn't understand why I was melancholy when I got back home.

"What happened?" Sherry asked.

"You just can't believe it," I answered. "You can't believe it." I couldn't tell her I was in a village that just got bombed.

So what does she say? "I'm going. Next time, I'm going."

So yes, she went with me. And she has been back to Sudan with me twice. When she would visit, she would talk to the women and connect with their stories. Everything I've gone through she's been through. She's been right there with me, step by step. She helped organize the demonstrations back in D.C., and even organized those five grandmothers who protested. My wife marched right along with us during the Artie Elliott thing. Just like you saw Coretta Scott King with Martin, you saw Sherry with me.

I did take some reporters to Sudan. I took talk show hosts. I took a contingent. There was a front-page cover story about this on *Talkers Magazine*. We didn't just go and observe, we took "sacks of hope." We took food, utensils, fishhooks, fishing nets and bed nets to keep mosquitoes away so people wouldn't get malaria.

As the former slaves came back after being rescued by Christian

Solidarity International, they didn't have anything. Their villages were so poor, they couldn't provide them with anything. We gave them sorghum seed so that they could plant food. We raised money through our listeners to provide these sacks of hope and distribute them to people.

We received threats from all over the world. I got phone calls from Canada, from Europe and from all over the United States that said if we kept doing this, they were going to kill me. But we just kept at it and kept at it.

Finally, in January of 2005, the war in Sudan ended. And when South Sudan officially declared its independence, I was invited by the government to the flag-raising.

GENOCIDE AND COLIN POWELL

We were trying to get the United States — specifically the George W. Bush administration — to declare genocide in Sudan. We arranged a back-channel meeting at the State Department with Colin Powell's chief of staff, retired Army Col. Lawrence Wilkerson. General Powell was not in the room, but that meeting came about because of him. Wilkerson said to us, "The secretary of state hears you. He's been following the demonstrations, and understands. I just wanted you to know that."

Then I ran into Colin Powell at a reception and he said to me, "Joe, you keep doing what you're doing, and I'll do what I have to do. But don't stop."

Next thing I know, he goes before Congress and utters the word "genocide." Once the secretary of state says it's genocide, it becomes official.

The next time I saw Colin Powell was at the raising of the flag in South Sudan. My wife and I were guests of the new government. It was the first time I had ever seen the birth of a new country. What a thing to see. People were there from all over the world, including the president of Sudan, Omar al-Bashir, who had been at war with South Sudan for 25 years. Everyone was there.

While there, I did an interview with General Powell.

"Now, remember, I was the first to declare genocide," he said to me.

"Remember that, Joe. Remember, it was me." He was so proud of that moment.

THE NATION OF ISLAM AND SUDAN

The Nation of Islam was definitely opposed to us, but I understood Louis Farrakhan's position. He had a relationship with Omar al-Bashir, the president of northern Sudan, which was an Islamic country. I didn't criticize Farrakhan, and to Farrakhan's credit, he never criticized me. But he knew I was going to do what I was going to do.

There was a Jewish guy, Charles Jacobs, the president of the American Anti-Slavery Group, who hated Farrakhan. He wanted to debate Farrakhan, so he used to prod me, "Well, why don't you go tell Farrakhan" this and that. "How come you're not jumping on Farrakhan?"

Literally, I had to curse him out. I said, "Look, you let me deal with Farrakhan. I'll handle it. I'll talk to the people in my community the way I want to talk to them, but you're not going to prod me into denouncing Louis Farrakhan. I'm not going to do it."

Jacobs wanted to make his name by taking on Farrakhan.

I told him, "You're not going to use me that way. There's some things I agree with that Farrakhan does and there's some things that I disagree with Farrakhan does. So I'm not going to be one of these Negroes that you're going to sit up here and prod into denouncing Minister Farrakhan. We just happen to be on separate sides of the issue."

In the end, the Nation of Islam's newspaper, *The Final Call*, attacked us and we defended our position.

I ended up, once again, on the right side of history.

CHAPTER 7

MY HEALTH SCARE

I had played football most of my early life. But just like most middle-aged people, I started gaining weight. Before you know it, I'm huge. I had ballooned to at least 275 pounds at 6 feet tall. Traveling had become painful — certainly during the Sudan trips, with small airplanes, cramped tents and lots of walking.

So I went to Dr. Gabe Mirkin, who offered medical advice on the air at WRC and was a good friend. He was both my personal physician and my wife's. My wife had to go in for an exam for a medical procedure, so Dr. Mirkin came out to say hello because I hadn't seen him for a while.

He stopped and said to me, "You're not leaving this office until I do an exam."

"Joe, I can look at you and you've gained so much weight that I'm willing to bet that you have high cholesterol," he said. "I know you've got hypertension because I've at least taken your blood pressure and I suspect that you're probably Type 2 diabetes."

He escorted me back to the examination room, took blood tests, took my blood pressure readings, came back and said, "Just as I suspected. You are Type 2 diabetes. You have extremely high blood pressure, and your cholesterol is totally out of whack."

Finally, he said, "I'm just going to be straight up with you. One day you're going to be somewhere demonstrating or speaking, and you're going to drop dead and nobody's going to know why."

He told me it was all environmental and weight-related. At first, I didn't know what he meant by environmental. I thought, what, am I breathing air that's bad for me?

He said, "No, no, no. You're doing it to yourself. You're eating yourself to death."

"There's a solution," he said, "and the solution is you gotta lose weight because it's all weight-related."

That was Dr. Mirkin. Straight, no chaser. And a great, great doctor.

"Here's the deal," he tells me. "I'm going to have to give you medicine to control your cholesterol, and I'm going to have to give you medicine for your high blood pressure, but you're going to have to take this. I don't care how you do this, but you gotta do it."

I decided to go public with my health issues because I know I'm not the only Black man running around America who has Type 2 diabetes and high blood pressure. I have always told folk I'm not going to ask them to do something I'm not going to do.

One day, I'm talking about it on the radio and I tell my listeners, "Man, I was taking more pills than Carter had liver pills."

Now, you may be too young to know what that is, but the old folks like my grandfather used to have these things called Carter liver pills. I don't know what they did, what they were, or if they were placebos, but they came in a little tin container and they were called liver pills. Folks swore by them. So I'm taking medicine for high blood pressure, but then I have to take medicine to counteract the high blood pressure medication. Oh my God. When I go back to the doctor, I find out that I now have to take insulin, so I have to be tested. I've got to prick my fingers.

I said to myself, "Oh, no. I've got to do something."

So I'm working out and exercising, but I'm still going to the big men's store to buy my clothes.

One day, Atlanta Mayor Maynard Jackson gets off a plane at the Washington national airport, starts walking down the concourse and drops dead. Exactly what Dr. Gabe Mirkin said might happen to me happened to him. Maynard had Type 2 diabetes, bad cholesterol, hypertension and big changes in weight. He dropped dead from what they call the comorbidities. That is when I decided I've got to really get serious about this.

About this same time, I ran into Jesse Jackson Jr., who had lost a tremendous amount of weight, and I said, "How did you do it?"

He told me his story: "I had a procedure out in San Francisco called duodenal switch, which in essence is a bypass. But it's not the lap band and it's not the stomach thing. They reconnect the intestines so that 50 percent of my food intake leaves me — it just flushes out."

Jesse said he and his doctors felt that probably was the best procedure, particularly for African Americans, since some people were having mixed results with the lap band. Al Roker had stomach stapling — known as the Roux-en-Y gastric bypass procedure — but his weight went up and down.

I was prepared to go out to San Francisco and have the procedure done, except I found out that there was a first-rate bypass surgeon here in the D.C. area. He was one of the best in the country, and an expert in the duodenal switch.

To qualify for the procedure, you have to go through a whole series of tests first. They don't just automatically do it. Then, I had to have a psychological evaluation, a circulatory evaluation, blood tests and more tests. I even joined a health club for six months to see if I could lose weight.

Then, we found out my insurance company did not cover the duodenal switch procedure. They covered lap band and stomach stapling, but they considered this other surgery experimental. Luckily, my doctor had been trying to find a case that he could take before the insurance companies, so we went to Aetna at the time.

Aetna told us, "No, we're not going to cover it, but you can appeal."

We went through the whole appeal process. We talked to patients who had gone through the same thing. It became a crusade. It really pissed me off that Aetna was willing to provide me with all the pills I wanted, but not the procedure to make them go away. That meant I would be taking pills for Type 2 diabetes forever.

I said, "So, here you've got a procedure that would cure me of these comorbidities, but you'd rather I take prescriptions for the rest of my life than approve this?"

We fought and fought them. Even the doctor got on the phone during the appeal process. But they continued to deny the procedure. We even went to the state insurance commissioner. By this time, my wife had taken the lead on this crusade. Then Medicare accepted it. They recognized the duodenal switch as a procedure. Once Medicare recognized it, the other insurance companies had to. That is how I was finally able to get the duodenal switch. Not only me, but now everybody else out there that wanted this procedure could get the insurance companies to cover it.

My doctor was happy, of course, that I got the procedure. The second day after the surgery, I'm in the hospital. The doctors and nurses come in with the results from my latest blood tests.

"Your cholesterol is normal and you're diabetes-free," he told me. "You'll never have diabetes as long as you live. And you've probably added 10, 20 years to your life."

The procedure is such that I can eat anything. I can even eat General Tso's chicken. With a lot of these other procedures, you can't eat certain foods, but I can eat anything. The only thing that I have to do is take multiple vitamins for the rest of my life to make up for the vitamin deficiency. That's it.

Before the surgery, I weighed almost 300 pounds. Now I weigh 185 pounds. I weigh what I did when I was a sophomore in high school. In fact, I have a photograph of a tuxedo that I owned when I was big. The tuxedo was so large that my wife and I could fit in it together and button it.

Rev. Jesse Jackson's daughter, Santita, got the same procedure. She was huge, but now she looks like a supermodel. Jesse Jr. told me that before her surgery, he and his father were very concerned about the health of Santita. That is when they decided that they had to do something about it. *Ebony* magazine did a story on my journey, and also featured Khaliah Ali — Muhammad Ali's daughter — and Bryan Monroe, who was then editor-in-chief of *Ebony* and *Jet*. They both had had similar procedures and were now living healthy lives, having lost so much weight.

Today, my doctor loves me. He's got more patients coming to him because of what I did with talk radio. What you hear is what you get. I'm going through what my listeners are going through, and they are going through what I'm going through. People listen. A lot of folks went out and checked out the procedure.

Many of them said, "I want the same thing Madison did."

I've got celebrity friends — I can't tell you who they are because it's a medical issue — who quietly did the same procedure I did.

They said, "I saw what happened to you and I went out and did the same thing."

Take a look at Al Sharpton. We thought Sharpton had had the procedure, but he didn't. Sharpton went the diet route. And it's funny because Sharpton said people were saying, "He must have AIDS. He must be sick."

Sharpton's response was, "Hell, y'all weren't saying anything when I was dying from obesity."

But I was morbidly obese. Your doctor has to officially say that you are morbidly obese to qualify for the surgery. That's how it works.

BATTLING PROSTATE CANCER

I did the same with my talk radio show when I found out that I had prostate cancer in 2009. I actually stayed on the air while I was going through my cancer treatment.

I learned about this when I was applying for a life insurance policy. They said if everything is normal, then we'll insure you. It wasn't.

I went to a urologist and he said, "Yeah, there's something going on there."

My PSA level — my prostate-specific antigen — was high. So I had to return in six months to see if it was continuing to go up. Guess what? It was going up. The urologist said he needed to do a biopsy, which is how we found out I had prostate cancer. In the meantime, I went ahead and told the audience once again that we got Black men dying of prostate cancer.

The doctor said, "Let's just play it safe and go get surgery. Let's do it."

So I told the audience, "Here's what I'm going to do. I'm going to walk you all through it. I'm going to keep you posted and I'm going to bring on experts."

Man, I found out there are more procedures for prostate cancer than there are Carter liver pills. There are procedures for freezing the prostate, for radiation seeding, for radical cutting and of course for removing the prostate. Oh man, there are so many procedures.

Well, I had a friend out in Palm Springs, Mark Hemstreet, whom I interviewed on my show and later worked with on an effort to try to have what he called a "mortgage holiday." Early in the Obama administration, while the country was reeling from the recession, Mark had an idea that Congress would ask lenders to allow consumers to suspend mortgage payments for one year to stimulate economic growth. The missed year would then be tacked on to the end of the mortgage. Unfortunately, the idea never went anywhere.

But Mark was also the owner of Shilo Inns, a small hotel chain. He told me a friend of his went to Loma Linda hospital out near Palm

Springs and had what they called a proton treatment. A proton treatment is in essence radiation, but it bypasses the other organs in your body. It's a lengthy process, like 60 days, because you've got to have quick-hitting protons directed right at the cancer cells. The actual procedure only takes five minutes. In fact, it takes longer to get undressed and dressed than it does to get the procedure. But like I said, you have got to be there for 60 days, every day, except weekends. I decided to do that procedure.

I had one doctor suggest, "Let's do the robotic thing," which is nothing more than a doctor with a robot doing the cutting. What I learned is that the first thing surgeons want to do is cut. That's what they get paid for.

I once thought about freezing. Then I even thought about radiation. The problem with radiation seeding is you can't be around children, which meant I wouldn't be able to see my young grandson. So I decided to go out to that hospital near Palm Springs. The guy who owned the hotel allowed me to stay at his hotel for those 30 to 60 days. My wife and I lived in Palm Springs for nearly two months.

I'd wake up in Palm Springs and do my show at 3 o'clock in the morning because it was 6 a.m. back on the East Coast. I'd take a nap after my show, then drive 45 minutes to Loma Linda, have my procedure at the hospital and drive back to the hotel. Luckily, I had minimal side effects. I experienced a little fatigue, but I would rest before getting up every morning to do my show, then drive and have my procedure. That means 45 minutes up, and 45 minutes back. In the meantime, I'm listening to SiriusXM radio and I'm doing my show, telling the audience, "Here's what I went through today. Here is the procedure, and here is what they did and how they did it."

I even had doctors on the show. I was doing my show around 3:30 or 4 o'clock in the morning when the lady calls from the front desk and says there's a Dr. Carlos in the lobby who wants to meet me. Now, I'm in this hotel suite that they provided for me, so we were doing the show remote. I was thinking, "Here we go. Some crazy or a fan is here at 3:30 in the morning because I don't know no Dr. Carlos."

Then the lady at the front desk called back and said it was Dr. John Carlos. Dr. John Carlos?

She clarified: "He said, Dr. John Carlos. Of the Olympics."

I said, "Whoa. You're kidding me."

It was John Carlos, who had been a listener of my show and knew

I was in Palm Springs. He lived in Crystal City, a little suburb of Palm Springs, so he just came by to say hello, since he was a fan.

It's like meeting a hero. I grew up with Tommie Smith and John Carlos — the two men who raised their fists in protest during their medal ceremony at the 1968 Olympics in Mexico City. Now here is Dr. John Carlos sitting in the lobby wanting to meet me. What are the chances of being in Palm Springs, getting cancer treatment, when one of the heroes of the Mexico Olympics just shows up?

Dr. John Carlos was one of the leading demonstrators, advocates and protesters of those games. I mean, he was the man who stood up on the platform and raised his fist with a black glove, barefoot. He is an icon of that movement, and there he was in the lobby waiting to meet me.

Of course, you know I interviewed him. And we have been close friends ever since.

CHAPTER 8

THE OBAMA YEARS

I suspect most people didn't think an African American could be elected president of the United States, and they certainly didn't think a relative newcomer who had the name Barack Hussein Obama could be elected president of the United States. And before he announced he was running, I was among those who didn't believe it could happen.

One of the most intense arguments I had was at a campfire in South Sudan with a young African American student from Harvard who was with us on one of our tours. He believed, I thought naively, that one day a Black man would be elected president of the United States, but I felt that was just youthful, wishful thinking. Now, this was before Barack Obama was a known entity, and we happened to be with a group of conservatives, so I thought that they were just playing mind games with this student.

They told him, "Oh, you know, America's not a racist country and one day, young man, a Black man like you can be president of the United States."

My response was, "Negro, you ain't gonna be no president of no United States. I'm not going to let these folks sit up here and fool you. America's a racist country and it ain't gonna happen."

The student said to me, "Oh, no, Mr. Madison. It will happen."

At that time, Barack Obama wasn't even a thought in anybody's mind.

I met Obama when he was a student working on Harold

Washington's campaign in Chicago. I was doing voter registration for the NAACP, and there was an organization called Project Vote. It was a grassroots organization that had received funding. Of course, we were all competing for funding from the same foundations to do nonpartisan voter registration.

Project Vote was headed by a young white guy named Sandy Newman. And one of his staff workers was a young guy everybody kept talking about who was really smart. This guy was *really* smart. He was a go-getter. And he was a Harvard law student. His name was Barack Obama. That's when I first remember hearing the name. And I remember later reminding the president about that. He kind of smiled and then said, "That was my first job, you know? My first real job."

But we really connected working on the South Sudan "Free Darfur" campaign.

He was a U.S. senator from Illinois at the time, but he already was thinking of running for president of the United States. And we were at the National Press Club along with George Clooney. Obama had already given his speech at the Democratic National Convention, and he was a rising political star. We were all together to talk about the rally we were going to have. I was emceeing the rally, so we exchanged cards. He was about to speak at this news conference and he wanted to make sure that I got recognition for the work that I had done before this in Darfur, which I thought was very decent of him. A lot of people don't give you credit, or don't recognize your work because they don't know how. But he knew.

He said, "I need to make sure I've got your name right and your title right. What years were you there?"

Then he made sure that folks at the news conference gave me the appropriate recognition at that time. And that's how we connected. Basically, we stayed connected throughout the campaign and even into his presidency.

I supported him when he ran for president. I tend to gravitate toward the underdog. I didn't have any real connection to the Clintons, although Hillary Clinton had also been very supportive of the effort in South Sudan and freeing Darfur. But I really didn't know her. I could relate more to Sen. Obama. And I also saw what they were attempting to do to him when he ran for Senate. People forget about that race. They forget how the Republicans were so desperate.

I'm thinking about Republican Alan Keyes, who in essence

carpet-bagged his way into the Illinois Senate race. There was controversy and a scandal with the incumbent, and then they couldn't find a replacement. For some strange reason they reached out to Keyes, who couldn't even win a Senate seat in his home state of Maryland. So he moved to Illinois and ran this terrible campaign trying to defeat Barack Obama. It failed miserably.

I was critical of President Obama's escalation of the Iraq war, but I understand that he wasn't a civil rights leader. He wasn't an activist. He was president of this big-ass corporation called the United States of America. He was leader of the free world, so he would have to do things and say things that people might disagree with. I come from the school of thought of Pastor Jeremiah Wright. Wright said to then-candidate Obama, "I wish you the best, but when you get elected president, I may have to disagree with you, I may have to come after you."

That happens in politics. I come from that school, so I reserve the right as a citizen, as a civilian, as an activist to disagree with you. This is why I've been in front of the White House picketing, particularly over minimum wage for federal employees. Also, I've participated in a panel discussion with these federal employees.

When you go to Union Station in Washington, D.C., it's a federal facility. The Ronald Reagan Building and International Trade Center is a federal building. The Smithsonian is a federal complex. There are restaurants run by vendors — there is even a McDonald's in the Air and Space Museum. This means the folks who own these franchises have federal contracts, but there are workers there who may be making minimum wage. Some employees don't have health insurance, some of them don't get vacation time and some don't get medical leave.

So, once again, we did a show on the topic. And then I did something about it.

One of the guests on the show was a woman who worked at the McDonald's in the Air and Space Museum.

She told me the manager allowed employees to have whatever was on the McDonald's menu for lunch. She saved her lunch to take home because she didn't have enough food to eat. If that wasn't bad enough, the manager found out that she wasn't eating her lunch at her appointed lunchtime because she was saving it to take home. So he told her that if she didn't eat at lunchtime, she couldn't have it. She couldn't take it home.

There also was a woman who worked at a Subway for years. One day, she cut her hand making sandwiches, and ended up having to go to the hospital.

It was a severe cut that required stitches. She paid $2,000 in medical bills, and she was off work for several weeks, so she had to take vacation time because she didn't have medical leave.

These people are, for all practical purposes, federal employees or contractors. These vendors have million-dollar contracts. So, the next time I saw the president of the United States, I decided to do something about it. In a face-to-face meeting at the White House, I told President Obama the same stories I just told you about these individuals. I also told him: "You are the landlord of these particular buildings, and these people are working in your facilities. You can sign an executive order right now that affects hundreds of employees, thousands maybe, across this country, not just here in Washington, but people working in national parks, people working in these same environments, people working in federal installations, hospitals, VA hospitals, all across the country. With one stroke of the pen, you lift these people out of poverty. One stroke of the pen."

We're in the White House, and I'm telling him that face to face. Now, the people around me are a little nervous because we were in the White House before the 50th anniversary of the "I Have a Dream" speech of the 1964 March on Washington.

I said, "Mr. President, in your speech, you should announce that you're going to sign an executive order to lift these people in the spirit of Dr. Martin Luther King Jr."

To his credit, he said, "We're looking at it. We're examining that. I've got my staff working on that." He didn't commit that he would do it in his speech.

A few months later, he did it. I knew he was going to do it when we were out front protesting in front of the White House, and he invited those same workers that I'm talking about inside to have a meeting. I told the demonstrators at the time, "You're going to get the executive order. He wouldn't have invited them in if he hadn't planned to do that."

A few days later he did it. That's what happens when you speak truth to power.

I'll give you another example. A ship in San Diego is being christened in the name of civil rights hero Medgar Evers. Everybody's there: his wife Myrlie Evers-Williams, Medgar's children, Vernon Jordan and Julian Bond. The night before, President Obama was in San Diego at a basketball game that was taking place on a military carrier. That meant President Obama was in the same city as Myrlie Evers-Williams, who was there to attend the christening of the Medgar Evers ship the next morning. The president never picked up the phone and called Mrs. Evers-Williams. Never called her. Big-ass mistake. The next day we were at the reception with the secretary of the Navy, and there were many hugs and kisses. It was a great ceremony and the first time I had been at a ship christening.

Myrlie and I start talking about the president.

In essence, she says, "I'm upset with him."

I said, "Wow."

Myrlie is something else. When she's upset with you she lets you know, but she wasn't making a personal attack. Apparently, she and Obama were someplace else before where he just didn't give her that recognition, and now he blew it again. I didn't have Obama senior adviser Valerie Jarrett's number at the time because I wasn't an insider. If I had been, I would have called the president and said, "Look, man, Myrlie's at such and such a hotel, and you're in town at such and such a hotel, so you should give her a call and congratulate her."

So, I was in a meeting with the president and all these talk show personalities: Tom Joyner, Michael Eric Dyson, Al Sharpton, Yolanda Adams, Doug Banks, April Ryan, Michel Martin and myself. So it got down to the president asking if there were any questions, and if there was anything he should be doing that he was not doing. You know, one of those kitchen cabinet advice meetings.

And I said, "Yeah, Myrlie Evers is pissed at you."

He asked, "What did I do?" And, it was kind of like a brother-to-brother talk, so we were all kind of relaxed now.

"Why?" I said, "Look, I don't know exactly why. I really don't know. But from what I gather you didn't somehow recognize her, or she felt snubbed by you. I don't know where it happened, I don't know the whole nine yards, she didn't get into detail, but I would say to you, Mr. President, that what you've got to do, and what you've got to learn is that sometimes all it takes at the end of the day is a five-minute phone call. That's all you've got to do."

Now let me show you how this all worked. Remember, this was just a conversation. I'm sitting next to Al Sharpton, so I said, "Now, maybe when they unveil the Martin Luther King Jr. statue, that would be a time to also give recognition to Myrlie Evers."

Al hit the ceiling. "No! Oh, no, no, no. That's the King family's time."

"You're right," was my response because I knew what he was trying to say. "Don't mix the two. Don't take away from the King family."

Now, to the average person what difference does it make?

In the back of my mind I'm saying the same thing, "Damn, come on. All I'm saying is also recognize Myrlie Evers. You've got the widow of one martyr here who's going to be here. Come on, man, you've got to make amends."

But I'm realistic because I'm a little older, and I understand where Al was coming from. Plus, you've got to realize there's a history there between the NAACP and the Southern Christian Leadership Conference that sometimes is contentious. But it was the Kings' moment and not the Evers family's moment. That was Al's position.

But Myrlie Evers eventually got the presidential attention she'd felt was lacking. Obama asked Evers to deliver the invocation at his 2013 inauguration, and he was photographed hugging her in the Oval Office.

So what's my point? You speak truth to power. Even though Obama didn't always do it when you want him to do it, he does it on his own time. Here I was making my case, telling the president what to do.

INTERVIEWING THE PRESIDENT

I have often tried to school some of my talk personality colleagues. Some of them had never been invited to the White House. Even though we know him as Brother Barack Obama, you've got to respect the office. You had to approach and treat him with the respect of the office. He's still president of the United States. He wasn't the Black president of the United States. He wasn't the president of the Black United States. He was the most powerful man in the free world. There were a hell of a lot of people who didn't want him in that position. So if you didn't show respect, they wouldn't show respect.

My take was this: "This is not a barbershop. This is not a fraternity house. We're not going to be sitting up here giving secret handshakes. When we're here, we treat him as if he was any president of the United States."

And let me tell you, the president was clever. My first interview with him in 2010 was not by phone, it was in the Oval Office. I know what he was doing. He understands the power of the Oval Office. Remember: I'm not in TV, I'm in radio. We got a call just before the 2010 midterms to get out the vote. The president understood the power of Black talk radio. So Sherry took the call: The president would like to talk about getting out the vote and discuss issues related to the 2010 election. And we said, "Sure," thinking we'd do it by phone. And they said no, come to the White House, and the president will do the interview in the Oval Office. So we get our engineers together, we take the equipment down there, and the president meets us and says, "Mr. Madison."

My response is, "Mr. President."

Now, we obviously know each other, so you'd think he would just say, "Joe, how you doing?" But I understand. The funny story is I had already told my wife and my engineer, "Don't call him Barack. Call him Mr. President. As soon as we walk through those doors, he is Mr. President."

So the president continues, "Thank you and come on in. Let's do the interview right here, this iconic position. You've seen it. The fireplace, the two chairs."

Man, you'd think this interview was made for TV. But I'm not doing TV, I'm doing radio. We mic him up, and this is the first time I've ever interviewed a president of the United States in the Oval Office. I've interviewed Bill Clinton, but not in the Oval Office. I've been to the White House on other occasions, especially when I was dealing with South Sudan during the Bush administration. So, this isn't my first rodeo dealing with the White House, but President Obama understood the power and the symbolism of that, and he knew we were going to have photographs taken. We were supposed to have only 10 minutes, but it ended up being 25 minutes.

Now remember, the president has got his agenda, and I've got my agenda. I'm going to ask questions, but one of the things I've learned with him is you've got to be able to interrupt him. You've got to catch him when he takes a breath because he's going to run his agenda, so you've got to be able to ask your questions. But I wanted it to last longer than those 10 minutes. The lesson I learned is the staff will give you their time, but that time doesn't count because the president will tell you when he's ready to end the interview. One of the funniest parts of the interview is that it ended with the sound of Marine One landing outside the Oval Office in the background. You can hear it on the tape. And we're talking, we're interviewing, we're going back and forth, when the president stops and says, "Joe, I've got to end the interview. My man, my ride is coming."

I mean, all of a sudden he switched into "brother mode."

He said, "Hey, Joe. My ride is here and I can't miss my ride."

It was hilarious. We actually left that in the interview. What president of the United States says, "My ride is here?" And that ride is Marine One, a state-of-the-art Sikorsky VH-3D Sea King "White Top."

Valerie Jarrett comes out and says, "Joe, thank you for coming. Appreciate it. We're going to get this right out and let folks hear it. We're going to get out the vote."

I have two funny stories to share about that interview. Today, we have an actual engineer, but back then, Don Wicklin, the program director, decided he was going to be the engineer because he wasn't going to miss this opportunity to go to the White House. He was all excited, of course, since it would be his first time. He was a white guy, and I always thought he was a Republican and not a supporter of President Obama. But he was still excited.

At the interview, he was nervous while putting the mic on the president's lapel, but I'm cool. At the end of the interview, we stop before we go out, and Don says to me, "You think we ought to check and see if we got the interview?"

"My man," I said jokingly, "if we don't have this interview, I'll fire you myself."

"What am I supposed to do?" That is what I said to him. "What the fuck am I supposed to do if we don't have the interview? Didn't you hear him? He's on Air Force One by now. What are we supposed to do? Run out there to Andrews Air Force Base and say, 'Oh, Mr. President, excuse us. We fucked up. We didn't get the interview.'"

Don stopped.

He said, "Yeah, I guess that was a stupid question."

I said, "Please. You got the interview."

The other funny story is about my wife, Sherry, who is also my executive producer. She goes just about everywhere with me. Now, remember, we're doing this interview for talk radio, but I have never seen so many people in the Oval Office for two people doing an interview. Who are all these people? That is why I say you've got to be careful because people are watching him. They're watching us. So, it ain't about getting in there, hand-shaking and fist-bumping and all that kind of stuff. Anyway, Sherry walked in and the president said, "Oh, Mrs. Madison, it's so nice to see you. You look so attractive today." He was very polite.

My wife said, "Oh, the drapes are just beautiful. So are the colors in the Oval Office."

I'm thinking to myself, "Only a woman would say this."

I mean, here she is in the Oval Office for the first time, and what does she notice?

The drapes and the rugs. However, President Obama is as smooth as he can be.

He says, "Michelle designed all of this. Michelle coordinated the colors."

Sherry responded, "Well, you tell the first lady she did a masterful job."

Then, as we were setting up, Sherry says to me in a whisper, "He's not wearing his wedding ring. Should I ask him why not?"

"Don't you dare ask him why he's not wearing his wedding ring. It's none of our business why he's not wearing it."

"Are you sure I shouldn't ask him?"

I said, "Only you would recognize that he's not wearing his wedding ring. What is this? Maybe it's in the bathroom. Maybe he got through washing his hands. Maybe he didn't put it on today. Of all the things, you want me to ask him that?"

The funny thing was, the next week on the cover of the *National Enquirer*, the president didn't have on his wedding ring. On the cover! And they showed the president's hands, he didn't have on his wedding ring.

Sherry says, "I told you! I told you, you should have asked him."

OUR RESPONSIBILITIES

Obama took some heat for his stance on personal responsibility.

In 2013, President Obama went to Morehouse College in Atlanta to give a commencement address. In it, he said, "Look, you've done your job. You're graduating. Now you've got personal responsibility. You've got to go out and do something. You've got to use this degree."

The president of the United States can't tell you what to do. He can't tell you how to use this degree in history or psychology or computer science. That's your responsibility, and you have got to be men. You've got to be leaders in your community. You have got to be good fathers. That means you have got to take personal responsibility.

People took exception to President Obama because the president was talking about personal responsibility. Conservatives like to think the narrative should be based on personal responsibility when it comes to Black people.

But liberals and progressives think it should all be about public policy. So when a president or somebody stands up and starts talking about personal responsibility, we take exception. Michael Eric Dyson takes exception when a person in a public position starts talking about personal responsibility because he thinks, "You're lecturing to us about personal responsibility."

I don't like that argument. I don't know why we get caught up in that argument. Of course, conservatives think that the downfall of the Black community and Black culture is that we don't take personal responsibility. But then the same conservatives refuse to finance and support public policies that are extremely important.

I always use the example that with public policy, you build public schools. That's public policy. But once that school is built and properly equipped, I have a personal responsibility to get my children up and get them ready for school, ready to go learn. That's personal responsibility. And public policy makes sure that they have a good school to go to, that they have books, that they have teachers. Personal responsibility makes sure they get their butts out of bed. It's a combination of both, not one or the other.

A lot of stuff goes on behind the scenes that the average person doesn't get a chance to be exposed to. That's where talk radio comes in. That's where these meetings with cabinet members come in. Talk radio is where we teach our audience about what is really happening.

I don't anticipate that Sean Hannity, the people at Fox, or those on conservative talk radio are going to tell Black folks what is really going on. So we have to do it. And some of these issues are very complicated. It takes me several discussions with different people to comprehend it. I'm not the sharpest pencil in the box, so sometimes I don't understand the complexity of an issue.

While we were playing checkers, Obama was playing chess. I'm playing checkers when I tell the president, "You've got to make this move at the Martin Luther King thing." He didn't tell me he is three months ahead of me. I wish he had, but he didn't, and he didn't have to.

He did as much as any other president for Black folks. But he still got beat up for not doing enough.

What I think happens is that we're used to having targeted programs — this program is targeted toward that particular group, this program is targeted toward that particular group. Sometimes, you do have to target a group. For example, the program with the boys, the My Brother's Keeper program, was targeted. But after it was announced, it caught hell because the women jumped in.

"Where was your program for girls? He's targeted boys, so where's the program for young girls?" My phone lines lit up.

"Yeah, that's a good question. I've got daughters. I've got a daughter, Shawna Renee, who does talk radio."

So then when I interview Valerie Jarrett, who is a frequent guest on my show, I raised the question. One of the reasons they come on my show is because they know I'm going to ask the questions. So Valerie told my audience, "How do you think the program for boys came about? Because we had a program for girls. Michelle was in charge of it. It was an identical program just to get coverage."

What it boiled down to was the program that Michelle had didn't get a lot of coverage. They had forgotten that program existed. That's why I said President Obama was playing chess while others were playing checkers. And Valerie told the audience, "That's how he came up with the idea for the program for the boys. He just duplicated the program that they had done for the girls."

That's the power of talk radio, of Black talk radio. My audience said, "Oh, oh. I didn't know that."

Not another call came in about it. That's what you didn't know. I didn't know. We were allowing all these bloggers and commentators to raise these questions instead of trying to find out the answer. Every month the secretary of labor, Tom Perez, would come on my show. He knew one of the first questions I'm going to ask him is "How come the Black unemployment is higher?"

Now, even though it was lower than it was when Obama took over in 2009, he answered honestly.

"It's not as low as it should be, but Joe, here is program A, B and C."

Most of my audience didn't even know his programs existed because nobody for the most part, certainly right-wing talk, was telling the audience that these programs existed. There were programs for IT, programs for unemployed veterans and a whole string of other programs.

And he says, "The problem is folks aren't taking advantage of it."

"The problem is, Mr. Secretary, folks don't know about it."

"Well, that's why I'm on your show." And then he comes back the next month and we got this bump of people calling and taking advantage of his presence.

There is an information gap. Information is power. But the personality has to be astute, knowledgeable, informed. It doesn't have to just be politics, it could be health, culture, anything. You just have to be willing to share the information.

One of the things President Obama told me in 2010 was that when he took over as president, the economy was in a ditch, and the motor was dead. So we got the motor started and pulled the vehicle out of the ditch, while the Republicans stood on the edge and just watched. We now have the economy sputtering along. We now have it moving in the right direction, but the Republicans want the keys back.

I always remember that car-in-the-ditch analogy about what President Obama did in those first two years. Had he not done that, we would have probably faced the second worst depression in this country's history. But the president always said we are not going to give them the keys back. And that's why people have got to go out and vote. He might have been able to push back more against Republican pressure if he had enough votes, but he faced too many constraints. If I had to fault the president on anything, I think he was too trusting, and not in a naive way. I think he felt that as long as he was honest, and did things by the book, things would work out.

But I think he failed to realize that when Republicans met on Inauguration Day 2009 and said that they would not cooperate or compromise with this president as long as he was president, they meant it. Their No. 1 agenda, in essence, uttered by Mitch McConnell, the Senate minority leader at the time, was to make sure President Obama didn't have a second term. I think the president didn't realize how serious the Republicans were. I think he thought that was just political rhetoric on their part because if you are a politician who has served in the Illinois Legislature and the U.S. Senate, you hear a lot of rhetoric.

The bottom line is you do have to compromise. President Obama had to compromise in the Senate; he probably had to compromise for years as a state legislator, so why would things change? But I think that the president failed to realize just how deep the racism went, consciously and most importantly of all, subconsciously. And I think that was President Obama's biggest fault. Either he didn't realize it, or he didn't want to accept the truth, but those crackers were serious, and they hid their racism well.

Years later, President Donald Trump proposed a $1 trillion infrastructure bill and it never got off the ground. Well, that was the same thing President Obama had talked about for eight years and couldn't get it past the Congress.

I quite honestly think President Obama should have been, and I hate to use this vernacular, but he should have been more cutthroat. The president went out of his way to avoid becoming the angry Black man stereotype that was made famous with the Luther character on the comedy show "Key & Peele." I think the president wanted to avoid becoming Luther, but Luther is in all of us. I mean, we all have to have a little Luther to maintain our sanity. The question is when does it come out? You have to be very strategic about it.

You know, President Obama navigated his way through Columbia and Harvard Law School and a racially mixed family. Growing up in Hawaii, Barack Obama experienced racism, so I think he certainly knows it when he sees it, but I think there were times when he should have just told them all to kiss his ass.

On the other hand, most African Americans did not realize what he was up against because we weren't part of the inner circle. We should have encouraged him to do more, and we should have said, "Brother, we got your back." We should have had his back more than we did.

We failed to realize we had to protect our investment, so we chose not to. We snapped back just like a rubber band and did not realize that these Republicans had not given up, they were still prepared to keep their promises, and they did. President Obama underestimated the resistance on the other side. And, we thought we had done something so outstanding in 2008, which we did, but we failed to realize it's an ongoing process. We didn't realize that this was not something that just ended on Election Day in November 2008. We had to keep up the fight. Stay vigilant.

Or we'd end up with someone like Donald Trump.

CHAPTER 9

TRUMP, OBAMA AND THE NIGHT IT ALL BEGAN

Saturday night, April 30, 2011.

This was the night, and we didn't realize this at the time, that President Obama gave the order to capture or kill Osama bin Laden. Turns out, he gave that order just before getting dressed to attend the annual White House Correspondents' Dinner with Michelle.

The dinner, also called the "nerd prom," was held at the Washington Hilton (the same Hilton where Ronald Reagan was shot in 1981) and was attended by 2,000 to 3,000 people. It is put on by the White House Correspondents' Association, and SiriusXM usually purchases two or three tables. It often draws politicians, TV anchors, celebrities and the D.C. elite. The president usually speaks, trying out his comedy chops on the audience.

It was President Obama's third appearance at the dinner, which celebrates the press corps and the people they cover, the political establishment.

Donald Trump, fresh off his "birther" crusade, was sitting in the center of the ballroom, just two tables away from me. And right in Obama's crosshairs.

Little did we know that President Obama had secretly given the order that same night to send Navy Seal Team 6 to Pakistan to capture or kill Osama bin Laden.

But that night, Obama was dropping bombs on the head of Donald Trump.

"Donald Trump is here tonight…" the president started in.

"Now I know that he's taken some flak lately. But no one is happier, no one is prouder, to put this birth certificate matter to rest than the Donald. And that's because he can finally get back to focusing on the issues that matter.

"Like did we fake the moon landing? What really happened in Roswell? And where are Biggie and Tupac?"

The crowd erupted. Trump just sat there, stone-faced. Obama kept at it.

"All kidding aside, obviously we all know about your credentials and breadth of experience. For example, no, seriously, just recently in an episode of 'Celebrity Apprentice' at the steakhouse, the men's cooking team did not impress the judges from Omaha Steaks. And there was a lot of blame to go around," he deadpanned, "but you, Mr. Trump, recognized that the real problem was a lack of leadership and so ultimately you didn't blame Lil Jon or Meat Loaf. You fired Gary Busey.

"And these are the kind of decisions that would keep me up at night. Well handled, sir. Well handled."

The whole place was laughing, and it was legitimately funny. Everybody at Donald Trump's table was laughing, one of these good old belly-type laughs.

The only one at the table who wasn't laughing was Donald Trump. There were thousands of people. Laughing. At Donald Trump.

He was pissed.

That's when it hit me. He's going to run for president. Donald Trump is going to run. For president! Trump was the butt of the joke and he resented it.

He'd show Obama.

Trump was now visibly uncomfortable. How DARE this uppity Black man turn his lauded career into a punchline. How DARE he!

And that's where it began.

I turned to my wife Sherry sitting next to me. We both knew.

Donald Trump was going to run for president.

Everybody underestimated Donald Trump. I mean, even the Republicans underestimated Trump. And they underestimated, once again, how deep the racism was, both consciously and subconsciously. In 2016, Trump had what some people refer to as a bandwagon. Let me explain this analogy. Like a bandwagon, everybody's got a different instrument, but they're playing the same tune. And the tune for Trump was: "Get Trump Elected." So, somebody played the clarinet. It might be David Duke. Somebody played the trumpet. Maybe it was the pro-life people. You see? They were all on the bandwagon playing the same tune with different instruments. Soon, "Get Trump Elected" became "Make America Great Again."

I think people fail to realize the extent to which support for Trump was driven by opposition to Obama. Even though Obama was not running, people still wanted to get him by going after his legacy. They were thinking, we're going to get him by beating Hillary Clinton. And despite what the leadership said at the time, I think it was an effort that incubated inside institutions like the FBI because I think there were elements in the FBI, particularly out of New York, who orchestrated all of that confusion in the end. The last-minute discoveries. The laptop that turned out to be nothing. There are no ifs, ands or buts about it in my mind. Trump had allies on the inside.

Now, look at the lack of enthusiasm, the anger and the stupidity of young white millennials who didn't get their way with Bernie Sanders in 2016. What did they do? Many refused to vote for Hillary Clinton. In doing so, they failed to realize that you don't win every election, but there are viable alternatives. You always have to recognize that there are viable alternatives. If they had taken that same enthusiasm they had for Bernie Sanders and applied it to Clinton after the convention, it might have made a difference. Yeah, so Hillary Clinton was not your first or best choice, but she was certainly a more viable alternative than Donald Trump.

The first day in office, President Donald J. Trump lied. He said more people attended his inauguration than attended President Obama's first inauguration.

It was a lie.

I did a broadcast from both of President Obama's inaugurations and had a front-row seat on the risers only a few feet away from the podium. In 2009, I saw the sea of people that filled the National Mall as far back as the Lincoln Memorial. The traffic was so heavy getting to our broadcast booth that we had to get out of the car and walk a mile because the cars could not get through. I had friends and relatives who actually had seats at the inauguration but they couldn't get to their seats because they were trapped in the tunnel trying to get to the Mall. There were a number of overhead photos that proved more people had attended Obama's inauguration. Trump's claim to the contrary was just a lie.

Donald Trump started his presidency on a lie and he's been lying ever since, and we have made a game out of it. The *Washington Post* started counting the president's false or misleading claims, and by July 2020 the tally had passed 20,000.

The trolls who call my show defending Donald Trump do not care that he lies. Some presidents lie for reasons of national security, but no president has lied 20,000+ times in just his first term. No president of the United States has lied as much as Donald Trump. I tell my audience that you just can't believe anything he says. You just can't.

You have to fact-check him, and one of the things I always try to remind these trolls and supporters of Donald Trump is that if they ran a company and were in charge of hiring, would they hire Donald Trump? Would you hire someone who was just a liar, whose word you just couldn't trust? The reality is that with him you have to fact-check everything he says. But that's the kind of commander-in-chief he was.

A liar-in-chief.

IMPEACHMENT

Trump was the third president in American history to be impeached (and he later became the first to be impeached twice). Many people do not understand the impeachment process, so we took the time on our show to explain it.

The House of Representatives voted in December 2019 to impeach on two charges: abuse of power and obstruction of Congress. The House was like a grand jury. It had to gather evidence and vote to charge him with crimes and misdemeanors. These are called articles of impeachment. The House can charge you with crime A, B and C.

The House votes, and if a majority agrees, they send the articles of impeachment — the charges — over to the United States Senate and the Senate holds a trial. The Senate itself acts as the jury. The chief justice of the United States, the head of the Supreme Court, acts as the judge and establishes the rules for the Senate proceedings. Each senator has one vote as a juror.

It takes two-thirds of the 100 senators to vote guilty in order to remove the president from office. The Senate did not find Trump guilty of either of the articles of impeachment. But history will record that Donald J. Trump was the first president to be impeached during his first term — not only once, but twice.

Richard Nixon was not impeached because he resigned before the House of Representatives voted on articles of impeachment. Barry Goldwater, the Republican senator from Arizona, had warned Nixon that he was going to be impeached by the House and that there were enough votes in the Senate to convict. On August 9, 1974, Nixon resigned to avoid becoming the first president to be ousted from office by impeachment.

But remember, impeachment is primarily a political process. And in 2020, the bulk of the Republican-controlled Senate supported Trump. It was purely political, as simple as that. We don't need to overthink this. The senators were more afraid of losing their seats than applying justice to the president. Trump has a great deal of support in the Republican Senate, and with the exception of Mitt Romney of Utah, Republicans did not have the courage to vote to convict Trump.

TRUMP AND COVID-19

During the COVID-19 pandemic of 2020, we discovered — or maybe we confirmed — that Donald Trump did not know what he was talking about. He's neither a scientist nor a doctor. He has the smartest scientists and doctors and researchers in the world to advise him. He just chose not to listen, and then decided to make up his own medical advice.

Coronavirus cases in the U.S. would be "down to zero" in "a couple of days," he said.

It's just a hoax from the Democrats, he said.

Take the unproven drug hydroxychloroquine, he said — it'll fix you right up.

We should consider using "powerful light" inside the body, or injecting disinfectants, he said.

Meanwhile, some 1,000 Americans were dying every day. And it continues.

Day after day, Trump was caught in a lie, and then tried to use Obama as a scapegoat. We all were in lockdown at home. I did my show from my kitchen.

Talk radio today is a lot different from when I first started in the business 30 years ago. We now have a system called Comrex, a portable "studio in a box," where we plug into the internet and do our live show from home. People listening cannot tell whether we're in the studio or at our kitchen island. In my house we call it the Madison Island.

Every morning I wake up at 4 and hook up my Comrex. Darrell Greene, my engineer, goes and locks himself into the studio. Our other producer, Sam Nassau, is at his home. We are in three different locations. We can still take phone calls and interview guests, and the phone lines light up as soon as we crack the mic. During the lockdown, people are at home watching news and listening to Trump's bad advice. One moment, the director of the National Institute of Allergy and Infectious Diseases, Dr. Anthony Fauci, says one thing, and then Trump says another. Ordinary people hear leaders discussing issues that are more important to them — Wall Street and the economy — instead of how people are going to eat or help loved ones who are stricken with COVID-19. The president talks about working people and infected people, but he emphasizes the economy and not humanity. There is also a stark contrast between Trump's news briefings and those of New York Gov. Andrew Cuomo, who has tended to lay out the facts with confidence and compassion. I think that's one of the reasons Trump's poll numbers started to decrease.

His popularity numbers started to go down among independent voters, because Gov. Cuomo was very clear. Cuomo discussed the impact it was having on families, the impact it was having on first responders. This was practical, no-nonsense information.

Trump, on the other hand, sounded like a very bad motivational speaker. He contradicted doctors and fed into nonsensical right-wing conspiracy theories. Trump played the blame game. He referred to COVID-19 as a "China virus" and did not condemn the theories that the virus was created in a lab in Wuhan, China.

Another major mistake by Trump during the pandemic was his support of the white protesters who viewed the stay-at-home orders as a tyrannical abuse of power. Trump pulled a Charlottesville when he referred to the Michigan anti-quarantine protesters — almost all Trump supporters — as good people. Trump incited rebellion against his own government's advice when he tweeted the word "Liberate."

As a civil rights activist, it pissed me off when white conservatives compared themselves to Rosa Parks and their ignorant protest to the civil rights movement. Rosa Parks sitting in the white section of a bus did not make people sick, and her protest did not spread a virus. What it spread was the civil rights movement. But what we were seeing now was not civil disobedience.

Civil disobedience is based on disobeying unjust laws, and you are willing to pay the consequences of breaking those laws. These protesters showed up with assault weapons. They had turned it into a Second Amendment issue. But why are they bringing weapons? Who are they going to shoot, the legislators? The governor? Their purpose was not to educate or motivate. It was to intimidate.

The refusal to wear a mask is similar to the seatbelt debates of the '70s. Even though everybody knew they saved lives, people back then did not want to be told to wear a seatbelt. Folks were dying in car accidents because they did not wear a seatbelt. People do not like government telling them what to do. The same with folks who do not want to wear a mask. They are like the folks who refused to wear a seatbelt.

Eventually, though, society comes around. It's about saving lives. The anti-mask or anti-seatbelt folks believe in rugged individualism and very limited government intervention. Before the Great Depression, the only relationship most people had with the federal government was going to the post office.

The protesters insist government cannot tell you what to do. Until you need government. I bet not one of the people participating in these anti-mask, anti-quarantine demonstrations have sent back their government stimulus checks.

In my studio, I keep a number of important quotes on the wall. One of the most important and popular quotes I use on my show comes from a collection of sermons by Dr. Martin Luther King:

"Nothing in the world is more dangerous than sincere ignorance and conscientious stupidity."

The first part of King's quote — "sincere ignorance" — is not knowing about an issue. Most Americans are ignorant of the political process. They just don't know. This is not a judgment. It is a fact. On my show, we try to educate folks about civics and politics.

I think if we learn anything from the Trump presidency, it's that Americans have devalued and, in some school districts, deleted the study of civics from the high school curriculum. Most Americans focus on the presidential elections but they do not understand the important roles of a governor or a mayor. For example, during the pandemic, Gov. Cuomo of New York and Atlanta Mayor Kiesha Lance Bottoms emerged as stars because they supported policies that kept their people safe. Cuomo gave great daily briefings and Bottoms told Atlanta residents to follow the stay-at-home order in spite of what Republican Gov. Brian Kemp wanted — to force the city to reopen.

Trump has claimed that he has unlimited power, but again, he lies. That is nowhere in the Constitution. Our system is based on checks and balances. That's why the Constitution gives the president limited power just in case the wrong person (like Trump) becomes president.

I try to explain how government works on the local, state and national level. Trump's presidency should reemphasize the importance of understanding your role as a citizen. The most important role we have in this country is citizenship, and that starts with voter education, voter registration and voter participation. Due to the pandemic, there is growing concern about voter turnout and voter suppression. Individuals are debating about the use of mail-in voting or in-person voting at the polls. Voting should not cost you your life.

We did a four-hour special, a town hall meeting titled, "The Vote Must Go On: How to Vote During a Pandemic." We interviewed the governor of Virginia, Ralph Northam, who was pushing mail-in voting. In April, he declared Election Day a state holiday. There were people who wanted to know if Trump could delay the November election. So we asked Eric Holder, former attorney general, if the president could delay a vote. (He couldn't.) We talked with the League of Women Voters and asked about the role of women and female Black voters. We held a four-hour civics course, not just about the importance of voting, but about how elections should work. What authority does a president have? What authority does a governor have? What authority does a mayor have? It's our responsibility to use talk radio to educate.

The second part of King's quote focuses on "conscientious stupidity."

Many of Trump's supporters, for the most part, are the embodiment of conscientious stupidity. I do not have a problem if an individual does not know. We can educate them. But when you know better and still lie, misinform people, push conspiracies and encourage people not to do the right thing, this is conscientious stupidity.

Donald Trump's refusal to wear a mask and listen to the advice of his doctors is conscientious stupidity. There is a relationship between power and symbols. Doctors say wearing a mask will help mitigate the spread of this disease. But the president of the United States, even with the outbreaks of the virus in the West Wing, usually refused to wear a mask in public. Trump was encouraging people not to wear the mask, despite knowing that it could save lives. He wanted them to practice conscientious stupidity.

King was absolutely right. Sincere ignorance. We can fix that. We can teach people. People can learn. We learn what to do to prevent the spread of the virus — wear a mask. But once you are taught better — once you KNOW better — and still refuse to do better, that is conscientious stupidity. And that is dangerous.

This pandemic is teaching us who our real leaders are, as former President Obama said in May. Obama must have heard my show when he said at a 2020 commencement address:

"More than anything, this pandemic has fully, finally torn back the curtain on the idea that so many of the folks in charge know what they're doing.

"A lot of them aren't even pretending to be in charge."

They didn't know. This was a test — there's the word. This was a test of leadership from the president on down to the school board member. It was a test of leadership. And Trump failed.

During the Great Depression, President Franklin Delano Roosevelt gave fireside chats in order to subdue fear and offer hope. But he also coupled it with New Deal programs, such as the Tennessee Valley Authority and Social Security. The federal government put people back to work, creating jobs to build the infrastructure that was needed in different regions of the country. The Hoover Dam in Nevada provided water for Los Angeles. The Tennessee Valley Authority provided affordable electricity to several Southern states. Social Security provided unemployment benefits and pensions for the elderly.

During this pandemic, when unemployment has become a national crisis, the federal government must invest in building bridges, airports, hospitals and roads, as well as increasing broadband capacity.

But instead, we're grappling with whether we can extend unemployment benefits and prevent a mass eviction crisis for people who can't pay their rent.

We Americans went to sleep. We did not see when Donald Trump started a revolution, so we found ourselves like Rip Van Winkle because we slept through it. We didn't see the Trump signs in rural America, on bridges and bypasses, on the sides of barns, on telephone poles and on pickup trucks. We just didn't see it.

We failed to see what was coming. The sexism. The racism. The lies. At one point in 2019, according to the *Washington Post,* Donald Trump was telling eight lies A DAY! But we still didn't see it.

I would also like to say this to my white, millennial, progressive broadcasters: "Will you quit acting as if this is the worst thing that ever happened in the history of the United States?" Come on.

The Civil War happened. Jim Crow happened. The Vietnam War happened. Trump's presidency is not the worst thing that has happened. And even if you think it is, then once again, what are you going to do about it? You have got to do more than just talk. My biggest frustration is all of this talking, which, you know, is strange coming from a talk show personality, but it's got to go beyond the airwaves. You don't accomplish anything just by talking.

Organize. Register. Vote.

What did the Trump presidency looked like? Well, the first thing I noticed was shock, then fear. And I mean shock from all walks of life. I've been at dinner parties with politically sophisticated people, former officer holders, journalists and their spouses, where they've all just gotten drunk. You know, they just drank themselves into remorse. This is a result of shock, that I-can't-believe-this-is-happening kind of shock.

Unfortunately, that type of shock leads to fear. So, after Trump was elected, I used my radio show to tell people it's OK to go ahead and mourn. I'll give you 30 days to mourn — 30 days to dress in black, weep and wail, do whatever you need to do. But after you get through mourning and complaining, you have to get organized.

And then do something about it.

CHAPTER 10

THE ACTIVIST

Over the years, I've used my talk show to participate in a number of worthy causes and raise recognition for famous Black entertainers, activists and institutions, from the Four Tops and Dick Gregory to the African American museum. We even visited Cuba.

THE WALK OF FAME: THE FOUR TOPS

Getting on the Hollywood Walk of Fame is an expensive process. Today, sponsorship fees cost at least $30,000. But first you have to qualify.

My friends, the Four Tops, presented me with a replica of their star on the Walk of Fame, but it didn't just happen. There was a friend of mine from Los Angeles who came on the radio show one day talking about how they were trying to get Marvin Gaye a star on the Walk of Fame. This was after Marvin Gaye had died. This friend was successful in getting Marvin's star. So, when we were in Los Angeles, I noticed that the Temptations had a star. The Supremes had a star. A few other Motown artists had one too, including Smokey Robinson.

Now, the Four Tops had been friends of mine. As a matter of fact, when I did work in Sudan freeing slaves, the Four Tops actually donated thousands of dollars to the cause. So, I noticed that there wasn't a star for the Four Tops.

We began an effort to petition the Hollywood Chamber of

Commerce, which is responsible for awarding these stars. Actually, the process of getting them a star didn't take long. It was a pretty easy effort, but you have to fill out a very lengthy application. There are several categories, including recording, movies, theater, television and radio. In some cases, individuals like Gene Autry have three or four stars because they're in television, they're in movies, they're directors, and maybe they're recording artists. So some entertainers had multiple stars.

Some people ask why this is worth the effort. Well, because it's history. It's not a question of just the recognition, but it's history. When you walk down the Avenue of the Stars, you look down and say, OK, who is Gene Autry? Or you ask, who was this famous director? Who was that person? These stars are marking history.

And we were able to do that for the Four Tops in 1997. They were so grateful to me, they named me the fifth Top!

THE WALK OF FAME: DICK GREGORY

Dick Gregory was like a father to me. I've known Dick since I was 16 years old. And despite all his years of activism, entertainment and humanitarian efforts around the world, Dick didn't have a star on Hollywood's Walk of Fame. But Whoopi Goldberg had a star, and Richard Pryor had a star. I could name a plethora of comedians who all credit Dick with influencing their career, but there was no star for Dick Gregory.

Our first effort to get him a star happened many years ago. I was still with Radio One, a local station in Washington, D.C. I found out that in order to get a star, you had to fill out an application, and then it was voted on by a committee. If the committee voted to award the star, you had to pay $15,000 at the time.

So I went on air and started asking people to donate money to raise the $15,000. The problem was I started raising the money before the committee voted to give Dick the star. That is why in the first round, they didn't vote for him. That meant we had to give the money back to people, or we didn't cash the checks that were sent to us. But in a few years, I decided to try it again.

By this time I was working full-time broadcasting with SiriusXM, which means my radio audience was much larger. And this time, when we reapplied, the committee voted to award Dick Gregory a star. They were going to give Dick a star on the Hollywood Walk of Fame. Amazing. But we came to find out that the Chamber of Commerce had raised the price to $30,000. That amount is for placement of the star and its upkeep in perpetuity.

So I went on the air, told everyone that we were successful, and that the Chamber of Commerce had agreed to give Gregory a star, but we needed $30,000. Guess what? We raised $30,000 in two weeks. In just two weeks.

And the money came in from a cross-section of people. Now, I started off saying, "Look, I know that there are 30 Black folk out here who love Dick Gregory that can come up with a thousand dollars."

And there were a few. Fraternity members challenged other fraternities to give. Truck drivers were sending $5 or $10 — those were the bulk of the contributions. And there were even industry heads like this man who was the only African American vice president of a major company in the Midwest. He decided to make a substantial donation because, he said, he heard Dick Gregory speak when he was in college, and Dick's words had influenced him in a very positive way.

But for the most part, the money to fund Dick Gregory's star came from little people, from working people who gave whatever they could: $10, $20 or even $100. In two weeks, we sent a check to the Hollywood Chamber of Commerce.

Then, of course, we went out to Hollywood. Now, the interesting thing is Dick's star is placed right near, and I can't help laughing about this, Selma Avenue. That was important to me because Dick made a comment about walking across the Edmund Pettus Bridge from Selma, Alabama. So, I just think where his star was placed is important too.

Dick Gregory should have gotten his Hollywood star 50 years ago, but once again, look at the power of radio. We didn't raise the money on TV. We raised it, primarily, from my radio audience. The night we unveiled Dick's star — Feb. 2, 2015 — a group of young comedians and entertainers came out, like the singer John Legend and his wife, Chrissy Teigen, along with Chris Tucker, who emceed the event. Some of Dick's old comedy writers were there as well. These were folk who had known him over the years. Dick's wife, Lillian, and his entire family were there.

People don't realize Dick was one of the richest comedians. He was the Chris Rock of his time. Dick was one of the top comedians — Black or white. Dick truly was one of the richest entertainers in the country, but he sacrificed all of that because of his involvement with Martin Luther King and the civil rights movement in the 1960s. Unfortunately, Dick was always told — and this is something he wrote about — that if he kept getting involved with Martin Luther King and the civil rights movement, certain venues weren't going to book him anymore. But Dick Gregory always kept on keeping on.

One of the things a lot of people don't know about Dick was that in my grandfather's hometown of Clarksdale, Mississippi, which is the Mississippi Delta, the Black folk there were registering to vote, but were losing their jobs, or being kicked out of their homes, and having to live in tents. So, Dick Gregory used his money to charter a plane to fly food and tents into the Delta for all those people struggling because they were sharecroppers, or they had lost their jobs. The sharecroppers were just kicked off the land, but Dick used millions of his own dollars, sometimes through performances where he donated all the proceeds outright to their cause.

And it's funny. What I've learned is that there are some people who know Dick Gregory, the comedian, but there are others who know Dick Gregory through the Bahamian Diet: the nutritionist. Then there are people who know Dick as the activist. And then, of course, there are people who know him from his lectures on college campuses, and those who know him as an author. The reality is Dick Gregory was all of the above, and, well into his mid-80s before he died in 2017, he was still writing books and still performing in comedy clubs, and still, yes, an activist.

52 HOURS STRAIGHT:
MY GUINNESS WORLD RECORD

Every February the good people at SiriusXM always ask, "What are you going to do for Black History Month?" Let's be honest. Usually, folks don't put a whole lot of thought into it, so what they do is record a daily Black history fact.

Now the reality is that on the "Madison Show" we celebrate Black history every hour, all year round, because for us Black history is not one month a year. So, I knew I wanted to do something more significant than record a Black history fact.

I wanted to do something out of the box, something different, unique.

I'm going to give credit where credit's due. About two months or so before February, Al Roker, the meteorologist for NBC, delivered weather broadcasts for so many hours in an attempt to break the Guinness World Record for a continuous weather broadcast. And they broadcasted, oh, it might have been 38 hours; I don't remember exactly, but he stayed on delivering constant broadcasts.

In the process, Al Roker raised money for some charity, so the light bulb went off in my head, and I said that's what we'll do. I'll do a continuous talk show broadcast to raise money for the construction of the African American museum at the Smithsonian.

Little did I know what that process would entail. First, you have to find out if there's a category, which we did. There was a category in Guinness World Records for the longest marathon hosting a radio talk show. The record had been, I think, 40-some hours, held by a talk show personality somewhere in the Middle East. And that particular talk show personality raised money for a young girl who needed surgery. So we knew we had a category.

Then it was a matter of finding out what the rules were, so here we go. The rules are that you have to have observers, different observers every four hours. They cannot work for the radio company. They cannot be related to the talk show host. You have to change them out every four hours. And I have to speak every minute. For example, if I interviewed Dick Gregory, as I did, or Aretha Franklin, as I did, I would have to interject my voice every minute.

This doesn't mean I have to give a dissertation, but I have to say something. And that's to make sure that I'm awake. You do get a five-minute break at the top of the hour. What were the other rules? You had to have different topics every hour; you could not just talk about one thing, but the host had to remain consistent.

So we decided we were going to broadcast for 52 hours — that's what we went for, and that's what we achieved, on Feb. 25-27, 2015. I have 30-plus years of talk radio experience, so we just called on everybody, but we had to be strategic about it. We knew we would get West Coast people in the late-night spots because they would be awake.

And I must say, no one turned us down. No one. Aretha Franklin said sure, I'll do it. Wayne Brady had never met me, but he said sure, I'll do it. When I asked Bettye LaVette, whom I had known back in Detroit, she said sure, no problem. Julian Bond, no problem. Eric Holder, no problem.

We interviewed athletes too, people who had never been booked on our show, but who started calling in. Then I'd recognize who they were and we'd interview them.

Our biggest problem was getting Dick Gregory out of the studio, because Dick was like, "You know, let's do it, baby."

He was as excited about the marathon as I was, so Dick came on twice. Dick Gregory appeared at the beginning of the effort, and then from 6 to 10 — in the last four hours heading up to that 52-hour break, there was Dick in the studio.

The interesting thing was the commitment of our audience. We had people who drove in from Dallas, Texas. I mean, they just got in their cars and drove to the studio to be observers. We even had folks who flew in to be observers. We were especially worried about who would observe at 2, 3, 4 and 5 in the morning. And you know what? There was a cadre of grandmothers who said they didn't have anything to do. They were fans of the show who said they would take the wee hours of the morning to sit in the studio and observe. They didn't even appear on air. And that went on for 52 hours straight. We raised over $250,000.

I'm certain we raised even more than $250,000 because people signed up to give on a monthly basis. Now, I can't take credit for this because I don't know if it's true or not and she never mentioned my name, but the day after our marathon, Oprah Winfrey kicked in $6 million more.

Everyone at SiriusXM, and I mean everyone, from the chairman of the board to the custodian, participated either on air, made an individual contribution or spent time taking questions. Everyone participated. I mean, that marathon was a beehive of activity. You have to understand that SiriusXM is a 24-hour operation with 150 channels. Now, I mean channels, not just shows. But we couldn't go off the air for this broadcast. If we went off the air for five minutes, it was over. So, we needed the engineers to be on duty because there was no room for error and it was as if this was the most important show in town. That is why I will forever be grateful for the effort that the company put in when it didn't have to.

And then, of course, the Smithsonian Museum and Lonnie Bunch, director of the new museum, were very grateful for our support. We were the only radio show to broadcast live from the dedication of the National Museum of African American History and Culture. We were right up there with the networks because Bunch gave us a place of honor to be right with President Obama when the museum opened in 2016.

In fact, we are featured in an exhibit within the museum that displays the microphone I used and the clothing I wore during the marathon. The certificate from the Guinness World Records people, photographs and recordings are all part of the exhibit.

THAT TRIP TO CUBA

This fact may surprise people, but only 42% of Americans have a passport, and fewer than half have used it in the past five years. As a result, these folks cannot visit any other country, not even Canada. This is the reason a number of Americans cannot name five countries in Africa — in fact, they think Africa is a country. Luckily for me, I have had numerous opportunities to travel and see the world.

In 2013, my wife, my team, and I had the opportunity to visit Cuba with former *USA Today* columnist DeWayne Wickham, who had been taking a group of individuals to Cuba for several years. He started off taking members of the Congressional Black Caucus and then he expanded it to scholars, journalists and students. He would go maybe once or twice a year under the auspices of education exchange. And he arranged for tours of government facilities, universities and medical schools, with scholars, dissidents and a cross-section of Cubans. Finally, my wife, who is the executive producer of my show, and I had the opportunity to go. So, I decided to try broadcasting from Cuba while we were there for a week. And what I didn't realize is that there had not been a sanctioned commercial radio broadcast from Cuba since the Cuban missile crisis, since America's embargo. There had not been a single independent radio program out of Cuba.

So, I got together with the people at SiriusXM, who agreed that this would be a project that they would take on. We proceeded to work with Wickham since he had contacts with the government. Engineers in Cuba and our engineers at SiriusXM had to talk to each other and agree to share satellite time. It was more than a notion because the embargo was still in place. This was nearly a year before President Obama went to Cuba, although we knew that it was going to happen. We knew that the president would be removing certain restrictions — restrictions later reimposed by Donald Trump. But the marvelous thing about it was, within two weeks, we were able to facilitate that broadcast with the cooperation of the Cuban government because the Cuban government runs broadcasting.

It was absolutely amazing. We ended up broadcasting at a radio station in downtown Havana in June 2015 — the first sanctioned independent broadcast done out of Cuba in over 50 years. In that radio program, we talked about Cuban culture and art. A few months later, the secretary of state announced that the United States was going to open an embassy in Cuba. Only a few months later, Obama would be the first U.S. president to visit Cuba since 1928.

The main thing is that through this broadcast, we got rid of many misconceptions, like the idea that Cuba isn't a safe place to visit. In fact, Cuba has exchange programs with students and a lot of other cultural exchanges. We also learned what young people who did not live through the Cuban missile crisis felt about normalizing relations.

So, we had an opportunity to interview students from Indiana and New Jersey. We even met Cuban journalism students. We learned from the journalism students that they really wanted an exchange program. They wanted to visit the United States, and they wanted American students to visit Cuba. But one of the most interesting things they wanted almost more than anything else was access to social media, because Wi-Fi is very limited in Cuba. So, students were really eager to expand the limited technology that existed there.

AMERICAN MED STUDENTS IN CUBA

We discovered that Cuba had made arrangements with the Congressional Black Caucus many years ago so that any American student who wanted to go to medical school could apply to Cuba's medical school and get free tuition and room and board for five years. And there were several scholarships in each congressional district that made this possible. Obviously, most people didn't even know this program existed.

One young lady we met was from San Francisco, and she had enrolled in medical school in Cuba. On the show, they all talked about their experience. For example, in their first year, medical students don't study medicine. They study the Cuban language. Of course that's the Spanish language, but it's a different kind of Spanish, so that first year is spent just learning how to converse. All the lessons are taught in Spanish, which they said is a challenge.

The second important part of their experience is that they go to school with students from all over the world. Since Cuba opened its doors to many African nations, Cuban schools end up educating medical students from all over that continent. Also, a lot of Chinese students study there. At least a couple hundred Chinese students a year end up going to medical school in Cuba.

The third thing medical students do is practice medicine in the communities. Students are assigned various neighborhoods or communities all over Cuba, so that is how they practice their medicine. Once they complete five years of their medical study, they are, I don't want to use the word trained, but these medical students are briefed and take classes on passing the medical boards exam. Cuba does that so that their students don't fail the board. That means these students come out not only ready to practice medicine, but if they return to the United States, they then are in a position to pass the medical board exams.

All the students we spoke to were very positive about their experience, and they never expressed any cultural problems, but you have to remember that they were hand-picked by the government to talk to us. They represented a cross-section of African Americans who came from Middle America and the East and West coasts. Medical school in Cuba was very rigorous training, and the students we spoke to planned to return to the United States to practice medicine.

We also met with Black intellectuals, Afro-Cubans who had created a study of race relations in Cuba. They told us that racism exists, even though Cuban officials denied that. One of the most heated exchanges we had during our visit there was with some people from the government, the equivalent of our State Department, who said:

"We're all Cubans here. Race is not an issue."

But Professor Mary Frances Berry, who was on this trip with us, really knew the history of Afro-Cubans and challenged the government spokesperson on that.

So there are no ifs, ands or buts about it. In Cuba, there is cultural racism and political racism, even though the government of Cuba wants to give the impression that racism doesn't exist. And we were able to shine a light on that.

CHAPTER 11

IT'S ALL HAPPENING SO FAST

2019 was one hell of a year. I celebrated my 70th birthday and it was my 45th year in radio. I received an honorary degree from my alma mater, Washington University in St. Louis, I was elected to the Radio Hall of Fame, I was featured on Henry Louis Gates' "Finding Your Roots," and I became a great-grandfather. Let me walk you through this incredible journey.

One day, I received a call from Mark Wrighton, chancellor of Washington University. He said, "I'm calling to let you know that the Board of Trustees at Washington University in St. Louis are awarding you an honorary doctorate degree; hope you will accept it and hope that you can be part of the ceremony." I was honored, thrilled, and didn't anticipate it, didn't know it was coming. My other surprise was that it was an honorary doctorate degree in law, so that's what surprised me. It was my first honorary degree. I can tell you that the whole family was excited, and we went to St. Louis with the children in May 2019 for the graduation. My children had never been on campus at Washington U. We took the grandchildren too, so the entire family was there. Former New York Mayor Michael Bloomberg was the commencement speaker, and he also received an honorary degree.

The dean asked me to give a speech at the Brown School of Social

Work's baccalaureate ceremony. I forget the title, but my theme was: Think big, but start small. They also must understand that their position as social workers is extremely important. I don't care how many degrees are handed out in medicine, science, history, law or economics. How people interact and how society develops depends on social workers. Social work is not about just welfare and just taking care of the underprivileged. I told the graduates that they must realize that their job is extremely important. My speech ended by saying that people are more important than possessions and principle is more important than power.

SHERRY AND THE STROKE

In January 2019, we were in the middle of a show and my wife, Sherry, who is also our executive producer, was in the booth with our engineer, Darrell Greene. She came into the studio and told me her arm was hurting. I told her to rest. She came back a few minutes later and said the pain had gone all the way down her leg on one side of her body. I immediately said it sounded like she was having a stroke.

I gave her some aspirin, because I had learned if you suspect someone is having a stroke you should give them aspirin, because it may break up a blood clot. She took the aspirin and brushed it off. She was having a stroke. Sherry went to the ladies' room and, fortunately for us, Laura Coates, host of the Laura Coates Show, the show that follows mine, was in the ladies' room.

"Sherry, something's wrong, you don't look well," Laura said. Laura told her to look in the mirror and Sherry saw her face was drooping. Laura said, "You are having a stroke." Sherry returned to the studio, I got off the mic and I told my audience we have a medical emergency and I must leave the show. I immediately got Sherry in the car and drove her to George Washington Hospital. George Washington Hospital was located across town, but I knew it had a special unit for strokes. On our way to the hospital, I ran some red lights and I was fortunate that there was not any traffic and I did not get pulled over by police.

In hindsight, I should have called 911 and have an ambulance take her to the hospital, but I was nervous and scared so I just said, come on, we are going to the hospital. Well, good thing we went to GW, because when I pulled up to the emergency entrance, the valet contacted the unit that deals with strokes, and in about five minutes six doctors arrived, put Sherry in a wheelchair and took her to the unit. I expected to be escorted to the waiting room, but they wanted the person who observed the stroke in the room in order to ask me a series of questions.

What happened, what time it was? How long ago was it? What were the signs?

They said the questions were standard procedure and they were preparing her for a CAT scan. All of this occurred within a half-hour, and the CAT scan verified that Sherry indeed had a stroke. I called the kids and the grandchildren. They dropped everything and came to the hospital.

Sherry stayed overnight in the hospital for observation, and the only physical problem she had was improving her balance. She came home the next day and I told her to rest, but the problem with Sherry is getting her to rest. She started to recover slowly. Her regimen included physical therapy and visits to the doctor. The doctors diagnosed it as a minor stroke and said what helped Sherry was that we responded immediately.

The whole issue with strokes is timing. You've got to get the person who is having a stroke to the hospital within 30 minutes. If it takes any longer, that's when you run the risk of paralysis and permanent damage. Sherry calls Laura Coates her angel because she recognized the symptoms in the bathroom. Laura even volunteered to finish my show.

The next week we interviewed her doctor, Christopher Leon Guerrero, a top neurologist at George Washington University School of Medicine, and interviewed Sherry in order to share her story and inform our listeners on what to do if someone is suffering a stroke. It reaffirmed that listeners appreciate the information because we are sharing our stories and they hear that we are people with similar issues.

Sherry had a year of physical therapy along with more CAT scans. She continues to see her doctors and receives steroid injections in her back. She has recovered without any permanent damage.

Sherry's stroke and my diabetes treatment were real-life circumstances and situations that address major health issues in the Black community. It gave us an opportunity to discuss the health care disparities affecting African Americans with conditions such as breast cancer, strokes, Alzheimer's, high blood pressure and diabetes.

It helps when there is a personality that they can trust and have developed a relationship with over the air. We get to spend from five minutes to up to four hours, or as much time as I deem necessary, to discuss the issues. I interview the doctors and any other health professionals. People get to call in, ask questions and share their stories. Talk radio is a great format to provide information to an audience because we are allowed to expand and create a community of shared experiences.

RADIO HALL OF FAME

For several years, I was nominated for the Radio Hall of Fame and each time I came up short. In 2018, I was nominated with five other individuals, and there were two types of votes I needed to get into the Hall of Fame. The first was the popular vote, where your listeners, fans, friends and families vote online, but the total number of votes did not matter because the selection committee counted that as one vote. If I received 1 million online votes, I received one vote for that category. The other vote was determined by 23 members of the nominating committee, all professionals in the industry.

I honestly thought that was where I was going to come up short, because the nominating committee is primarily composed of conservatives. This is just the nature of talk radio. Conservative talk dominates almost every aspect of talk radio. The top five talk show radio programs in America are conservative. But in the summer of 2019, I received a call from the chair of the nominating committee saying I had received all 23 votes. I must say, I was floored and really surprised. When you think about some of the folks, it was a heck of a group of people, including Stephanie Miller, a veteran liberal talk show personality, and Suzyn Waldman, the first voice heard on WFAN in New York, the first 24-hour sports talk show in the nation. If I were Suzyn, I would have told the fans at Yankee Stadium to vote for me and they would receive a free hotdog.

The Radio Hall of Fame event took place on Nov. 8, 2019, at Carnegie Hall in New York City.

During my acceptance speech, I demanded that the Radio Hall of Fame committee have more African American radio hosts and other people of color. In fact, during the speech I said there was no way I was going to accept this honor over people like Donnie Simpson, former video DJ on Black Entertainment Television, and Sway, host of "Sway in the Morning" on Shade 45 on SiriusXM. Two weeks after the Hall of Fame ceremony, I received a phone call from the Hall of Fame nominating committee asking me to serve on the committee. During our first meeting I said SWAY should be at the top of the list. One year later, half of the Hall of Fame inductees were talk radio hosts of color — a first in the history of the Radio Hall of Fame.

I was very surprised to receive a unanimous vote. I attributed the vote to my consistency in talk radio and the number of issues that we encouraged our audience to support. For example, my show was live on the air for 52 consecutive hours, winning a world record and raising over $250,000 for the Smithsonian African American museum. I traveled to South Sudan during its civil war and freed thousands of slaves. I was diagnosed with prostate cancer and gave a live broadcast during my treatment to encourage Black men to get checked and treated for prostate cancer. We traveled to Haiti after Hurricane Matthew and raised money for Haiti. We have participated in a number of voter registration drives, and what I tell my colleagues is that our show is more than just talk. You can change the world with the spoken word, but as I remind my listeners, I did not receive these honors by myself — it takes a team.

I don't care if it's the hall of fame of Major League Baseball, football, basketball or even golf, but you have to have a good caddy. The reality is that it takes a team and that's why you always hear me say this is not just an individual honor.

Like I said, 2019 was a great year, and then to cap it off, I became a great-grandfather. My granddaughter had graduated from the University of Wisconsin, then moved to a Native American reservation in South Dakota to teach elementary school. She had previously spent her summers working with children near there. She and her partner had a daughter in the spring of 2019.

FINDING YOUR ROOTS

Years ago, Professor Henry Louis "Skip" Gates Jr. asked me if I would be interested in being part of the "Finding Your Roots" program, in which Gates and a team of researchers conduct a deep dive into your family history using DNA and historical records. I told him yes, absolutely. It's a very popular program, so I told him yes. Some years go by and every now and then I run into Skip at Penn Station in New York and he would try to avoid me so I would not ask him anything about his research into my family tree. I asked Skip, "Hey, brother, when are you going to finish the 'Roots' thing? What's going on? Can't be going that far back." He'd laugh.

In early 2019, Gates called me one Saturday morning and said, "I've got good news and I've got bad news, so which do you want first?"

I said, "Well, what's the good news?" He said, "We finished the series. We finally finished. We're ready to record." I said, "Well, then what's the bad news?"

"The man you know as your father, Felix Madison, is not your biological father." There was the pause, and he said, "I'm obligated to tell you this. We can't just surprise you with it when we record the interview."

He told me he had surprised LL Cool J, and it was a disaster. LL Cool J was very upset when Gates told him that LL's grandmother was not his biological grandmother. Gates thought LL was going to knock him out, so they came up with a policy and now Gates informs all guests of any family secrets before they air on the show.

Gates said, "It's up to you, and the reason I'm calling you is that even though we've done five years of research, you don't have to do the program." I thought that was interesting, because that's a lot of time, money and resources, and he said, "But that's up to you, and I won't hold it against you."

The questions I had ... well, I knew that Felix Madison wasn't alive. He had died some years ago. My mother and most of my immediate family passed away when I was in my 20s. I said, "Well, is the biological father still alive?" He said, "No. He just passed away."

He passed away, I think, in 2000, he told me, and he said, "And I also have to tell you, you have two half-brothers." Wow. And then he went on to say, "One of the half-brothers lives in Los Angeles. He's the younger. You're the middle boy, and the older half-brother is from Dayton, Ohio, and grew up with you, went to the same elementary and high school and lived on the same side of town."

Gates said, "Now, we haven't told them that they're related to you. You know who they are, but they don't know. We've notified them, but they don't know that it's you." I said, "No, let's go. Let's go ahead." It is what it is. I joked with him and said, "If you had called me just a half an hour ago, I just hung up from a cousin who is Felix Madison's nephew, and he just borrowed $1,500 from me, man, and if you'd called me half an hour ago, I could have told him, 'No, I'm not loaning you. You're not related to me.'" I said, "The only reason I gave it, because he's a favorite cousin of mine."

I laughed, and he said, "Oh, you wouldn't have not done that," and I said, "No, I would have given it to him." Of course, he hasn't paid me back, either.

We did several promotions for Gates' PBS special, and the show was held at Lisner Auditorium in Washington, D.C., and aired in April 2019. There were between 1,800 and 2,000 people in the audience, with Skip moderating the panel. They showed the trailers from my episode, and my entire family was in the audience when they showed me a photo of Felix Madison.

Skip asked me, "Do you know who this is?" I said, "Yeah, that's my father, Felix Madison."

Then he said, "All right, now turn the page." And I turned the page, and they had the first photograph I've ever seen of my biological father. And they showed his picture on the screen in the auditorium, and I literally could hear the audience gasp, because people saw the immediate resemblance.

My real father was named Herman Haygood, and he was from Dayton, Ohio. Apparently, he left Dayton and moved to California, and that's where he ended up living most of his life. What I learned about him was that he was a very industrious individual, an entrepreneur who bought homes, renovated them and then resold them. He was said to be the go-to person when other people needed cash. He apparently died of prostate cancer, somewhere around the year 2000.

I have no idea how Haygood met my mother, or what kind of relationship they had, though it would appear that it was somewhat intimate. I don't believe that Felix Madison ever knew that he was not my real father. Although he did abandon me when I was very young, he later treated me like I was his son. My sister, Yvonne, and I used to spend summers with him in Flint, Michigan, where he worked at the Buick factory. Felix Madison came to my first wedding, and he was the only person in my family who drove down to my graduation from college at Washington University in St. Louis.

Many people have asked me how it felt when I saw my biological father. I didn't have any raw emotions and I was not upset. We don't choose our family but we do choose our friends, and this was my attitude after I found out about my biological father. I didn't have any choice who my biological parents were, but I can decide who are my friends.

Much of this PBS show focused on my biological father's side, and it turned out that his father was part of the Tuskegee Syphilis Study. During the 1930s, white scientists believed that Black men responded differently to syphilis. My grandfather was a Black man with syphilis that was left untreated to see the long-term results.

The only grandmother I knew was Betty Stone, the second wife of my maternal grandfather, Jim Stone, the prizefighter. My biological grandmother was actually Jim's first wife, Ethel Waters, who gave birth to my mother, Nancy, or Nan for short. I learned from this "Finding Your Roots" program that Jim Stone tried to divorce Ethel Waters a couple of times, and I don't know what was going on with them. But he soon married Betty Lou Johnson, who became Betty Stone, and she raised my mother, Nan Stone.

Betty Stone was not my biological grandmother, but she was the only grandmother I knew. She was always "Mama," and I don't know what happened with my parents, but I am proud to say that I was raised by my loving grandparents.

Before "Finding Your Roots," whenever I gave a speech or made appearances in Moss Point, Mississippi, Felix Madison's family would come to my talk and we would catch up with each other. There was a whole group of them before the PBS special who lived near Moss Point. They are from Gulfport, because Felix Madison grew up in Rosedale, somewhere between Hattiesburg and Moss Point. They were happy to introduce me as their cousin. After the PBS series, when they found out that Felix Madison was not my biological father, I have not received a single phone call from those folks.

The only one I've been in contact with is the cousin who owes me $1,500.

THE PAST IS NOT PAST

I was speaking to a young activist in Detroit and like many young people he said, "It is time for the older generation to pass their torch to the younger generation." In fact, I said that back in Detroit in the 1970s, when I led demonstrations in that city. I still hear this today among young freshmen in Congress who say the older people in Congress have to pass the torch.

Recently, I gave a speech, and I said, "I used to say it's time for the older generation to pass the torch to the younger generation." But I told the audience, "I am not going to pass my torch to you, but I am going to light your torch." This is a new way of thinking, a new attitude, because if I pass my torch to you, it leaves me in the dark, but if I light your torch, we can both see and move forward together.

Let me tell you, that comment resonated, and I gave that same speech to a group of Congressional Black Caucus members down in Tunica, Mississippi. Benny Thompson, Jim Clyburn and Maxine Waters attended my talk and a number of young people. I received a loud ovation for my comments.

In 2019, I attended the NAACP convention in Detroit. The NAACP has had a long history of younger generations telling members of older generations to pass the torch. I served on the NAACP Board for 14 years but was rejected twice to serve as the NAACP executive director, but then I am asked to speak at their membership luncheon in, of all places, Detroit. During the speech, it was the first time I use that line: You all quit talking about passing the torch. I'll light your torch, and then we can both move forward together. My torch isn't going out until I die.

Julian Bond and Benjamin Hooks lit my torch. These were folks who lit my torch and allowed me to go forward, but they held onto their torch. They didn't give up. They didn't stop. They didn't extinguish their torch.

The reaction of the audience was visceral from both young and old. After my speech, Maxine Waters came up to me and said, "You are absolutely right. You are absolutely right," and some of the younger members, the freshmen in the caucus, came up and said, "You're right."

The previous year, on Nov. 1, 2018, SiriusXM put on a live broadcast at the Apollo and there was a panel with Michael Steele and a group of SiriusXM personalities from Progress and Urban View. Al Sharpton and Karen Hunter, radio hosts on Urban View XM Sirius 126, co-hosted the event. The panelists talked about voting and holding candidates accountable. This was the first time I took the stage at the Apollo, and I was excited and considered it a big deal. Here I am on the stage at the Apollo. The place was packed. SiriusXM listeners and subscribers, and we get into this discussion about politics and generational tensions between the millennials and the baby boomers.

One of the millennials on the panel said the baby boomers need to move on. And then it was my turn to speak, and I said, "Let me tell you something. We gave you Negroes the right to vote. We gave you millennials the right to vote. We died for this. The fact that you are on the stage and you have this radio format, you have the right to vote, quit playing into this Willie Lynch attitude," because that's what they want us to do. They want millennials to go against baby boomers, and I'm not going to play that game.

Man, the audience went wild. Sherry was in the audience and she heard what people were saying: "Drop the mic, Joe, drop the mic." It was one of those drop-the-mic moments, and so I kind of laughed with my wife when we were heading back to the hotel. She said, "In your own way, you won the crowd over in the Apollo, like winning amateur night at the Apollo." But I ain't no amateur.

In the audience was a producer from "Morning Joe." The next week the producer called me and asked if I would go on the "Morning Joe" Show, and at first I said sure, thinking it was something that could be done remotely. But then it turned out they wanted me to leave my studio in Washington and travel across town to the NBC studio and interact with him on his show live in the morning — at the same time I was supposed to be doing my show.

I said, "Hell, no." Think about it. They wanted me to interrupt my show to come on their show. They continued to ask for several weeks and the producer said to me, "Don't you realize this is TV? This is 'Morning Joe.' This is TV."

I said, "No, I'm not going to do that." What does that say to my audience? I leave my audience in the middle of my show to do his show on MSNBC. I don't know this for a fact, but I bet you there are more people listening to me in the morning in their cars than are sitting at home watching television. Most people, at 6, 7 or 8 in the morning, are going to work. They're not watching TV. I said, "No, I'm not going to do it." They could not understand why I would not do that. I realized that it did not make sense to go on his show in the morning and neglect my audience. To be quite honest, I think it's an insult to my audience, as if I think more of his audience than I think of my listeners.

To SiriusXM's credit, the management said, "I'm glad you told them no." They never encouraged me to do it; they said it was up to me. I said, "No, I'm not going to do it." I said, "If anything, why don't they put a camera and we can simulcast back and forth?"

You protect your brand. They wanted me on a regular basis, and even if they were going to pay me, I still would have refused to do the show because my audience and my brand is just as important to me as it is to their brand. Why would I undervalue my brand and my audience to go on their show?

People think TV's king and to be quite candid, when I initially started going on TV, I did it for the exposure. That's why a lot of talk personalities were going on TV, but when we looked at the ratings, more people listen to the radio than watch television. So I'm thinking, who's helping who? My audience gets to experience my show. Their audience gets to experience my show. It's a quid pro quo, but quid pro quos have their value, and it's all a cycle, because if you notice now, you don't see any talk personalities on any show. What do you see? Mostly politicians and lawyers and journalists.

THE SWEAR JAR

I got the idea of the "swear jar" from a comedian who had a gimmick that every time he swore, a bell rang. This comedian was on the air, and each time he swore, he was fined. And he said OK, he would pay the fine. We have to understand that media and broadcasting are very different today than during the George Carlin era and his famous "seven words you can't say on television."

I was listening to a Howard Stern broadcast on SiriusXM — remember, where we can say just about anything — and some woman pissed Howard off. She didn't like what Stern did on his show. Now, anybody who listens to Howard Stern knows he doesn't give a damn. That's part of his shtick. Howard lit into this woman with a string of profanity, and I said, whoa. Now, on SiriusXM, we have regular comedy channels, tame, PG-rated. Then we have adult comedy channels — this is your Eddie Murphy and Richard Pryor, grown folks comedy. Howard tends to fall into the latter category.

One afternoon, I was with our president and chief content officer, Scott Greenstein, and we were having a general conversation about the future of my show. We talked about what we are doing right and what improvements we should make. I mentioned to him that I had heard Howard just curse a woman out. Then I asked, "Can I do what Howard does?" He said, "Well, I've heard you curse on air." I said, did it bother you? He said, no, not really, because it was organic. He said, no, I don't have a problem with it. How could I? Howard does it and folks do it on the different channels all the time. The callers do it, too.

I said, OK, fine. Now I laughed, because I did point out to him, it's one thing for a white guy like Howard to curse somebody out, but will you have my back if I end up cursing a white person out? They may call in, tweet or send an email to complain, and he said, of course, we have your back. If Howard can do it, you can do it. What added a twist to this is that I had a caller who would be offended if I cussed. The caller said, "Mr. Madison, you shouldn't talk like that. You shouldn't use those words." Usually, it's elderly people who complain. Or a parent will call in and say there are kids listening to your show.

I was giving a speech in San Francisco and after my talk a mother and her 14-year-old daughter gave me a swear jar. She said, "We listen to the show every day, and my daughter actually made it." It was a fancy jar, like a vase, with little designs and the words "SWEAR JAR" written on the front. When I told comedian George Wallace that I had a swear jar, he said, "Black folks don't swear, they cuss."

I put a dollar in every time I cussed, and then I told the audience, at the end of the month, I'm going to donate whatever's in the cuss jar to a nonprofit organization. I donated the money from the swear jar to several charities, including the African American museum at the Smithsonian, the Red Cross, and the Trayvon Martin Foundation.

During the pandemic, I donated money to Feeding America. But the irony is, whenever I go out to speak, the people line up to take selfies and get autographs, and people hand me $20 and $10 bills for the cuss jar. At Morehouse College, I participated in a town hall meeting on the importance of voting and people lined up to shake hands and take selfies and I walked out with over $400 in cash for the swear jar. Some of the money even came from ministers.

I was at an Apple store, just getting a new device, and Sherry and I saw a young man who recognized me. He came up and said, "Mr. Madison, I really enjoy your show and I listen all the time." He handed me his card, which I put in my pocket. He is in the military and when he came back from oversees, he said, "Oh, I forgot," and he gave me a $100 bill for the swear jar and said, "This is my contribution to the swear jar."

People are living vicariously through me and the show. Maybe you can't swear on the job, or you're a minister (I always laugh, because I always tell my minister friends some of the best curse words I learned were from ministers). It doesn't matter.

Every now and then I may feel a little guilty for cussing and I tell myself to just stop swearing. In all honesty, the swear jar is a gimmick and I tell people, the cussing makes me feel like I'm channeling my inner Samuel L. Jackson. One day I put the question to the audience: Should I just retire the swear jar? The majority of caller said no, do not give it up.

My staff and SiriusXM said I shouldn't eliminate the swear jar. There are 200 channels on Sirius and you are likely to hear anything. I have heard some of our hosts on the comedy shows talk about things that wouldn't even cross my mind to discuss on air, and they are never asked to stop. What convinced me to keep the swear jar is after I heard Sen. Kamala Harris in an open forum say, "What the fuck is that about?" or when I heard former National Security Advisor Susan Rice drop the F-bomb.

Donald Trump is on tape talking about grabbing pussies. Our show is an adult show and one can listen to each episode on demand if they do not want their children to hear me cussing. But I'm gonna cuss.

When I cuss, it is not gratuitous. It is organic. I do not cuss for the sake of cussing. I've had folks who have called up and insulted my race. People have called up and insulted my wife. In those case, I will very organically say "F-U!" Usually it comes out without thinking about it, because I don't have to think about it. I'm going to be honest in how I feel, and I think that's what makes my show different. I think that's why people have told me not to give it up. It's honest, unfiltered, and I think that is what people appreciate. People want authenticity.

As a child, one of the first poems I memorized was Rudyard Kipling's "If." The last stanza is how I have tried to live my life:

If you can talk with crowds and keep your virtue,
Or walk with Kings — nor lose the common touch,
If neither foes nor loving friends can hurt you,
If all men count with you, but none too much;
If you can fill the unforgiving minute
With sixty seconds' worth of distance run,
Yours is the Earth and everything that's in it,
And — which is more — you'll be a Man, my son!

All people count, and no one counts too much, because we are all human, and that's how I have tried to deal with people. I have met queens and Supremes, presidents and porters. People of all walks of life all count, but none count too much. I've always been told that you always treat people how you would like to be treated. My grandparents used to tell me, be careful how you talk to people, because the same people you meet going up in life are some people you might meet coming down. This is how I try to live my life, and so far it has worked.

CHAPTER 12

A MOMENT OR A MOVEMENT

....

There it was, right in front of us.

Young people. Taking to the streets in numbers I hadn't seen in decades.

As Sherry and I sat in our living room in Washington, D.C., in June 2020, and watched CNN, the scenes in Minneapolis and New York, Oakland and Seattle and, just a few miles away, in front of the White House, this time it felt different. We didn't know at the time we were witnessing what the New York Times showed was, in fact, the largest protest movement in U.S. history. But still, we knew it was different.

These young men and women – Black, white, Hispanic, of all races and genders – were literally rising up before our eyes. There was a passion, a relentlessness, a commitment that I hadn't felt in years.

They had no leaders, no central organizing body as far as I could tell. They had no Reverend Al Sharpton. No NAACP. And that was a good thing. Without a centralized leader, who are you going to target? Who are you going to assassinate? Whose job are you going to take away? Whose family are you going to threaten?

They were decentralized, but even more powerful. They had a new way to communicate. Their word-of-mouth did not come by way of Freedom Riders or the 6 o'clock news, but instead it was on Twitter and Instagram, in text messages and on group chats.

And they were all united.

They had all seen the 9 minutes and 29 seconds of cellphone video. They bore witness as the white Minneapolis police officer, Derek Chauvin, knelt with his knee crushing George Floyd's windpipe. They heard George Floyd beg for his life — "I can't breathe" — and cry out for "Mama." They watched as the final gulps of air were squeezed out of George Floyd's lungs, never to return.

This time, it was just too much.

You see, I know protests. I've marched on the streets of Detroit, battled for the rights of Black workers. I been thrown in jail with Dick Gregory while we fought to expose the CIA and its involvement in the crack cocaine epidemic of the 1980s. I've been beaten, shot at, intimidated and threatened with my life. All just to make a difference. We were telling America that Black Lives Matter long before they thought to put it on a T-shirt.

Fifty years ago, that was me out there, leading others, fighting for justice. But 50 years ago, we weren't also battling a global pandemic that was killing Black people at rates more than twice those of white people. And 50 years ago, we didn't have a racist, narcissistic megalomaniac who literally lied every day in the White House (at least not one as bad as President Trump). Sure, we had Watergate, and redlining. We had riots and lines at gas stations. We had rampant racism and unchecked sexism. But this time, something felt different.

So, as we watched in disbelief on June 1 while the president of the United States ordered federal officers to tear-gas peaceful, unarmed citizens exercising their constitutional rights IN FRONT OF THE WHITE HOUSE, I started to wonder out loud: Is this just another disruptive spasm in our nation's slow crawl along the bending arc of justice, or is this a real inflection point, where a nation unites and things will never be the same?

Is this a moment or a movement?

The question mattered to me greatly. I had spent most of my adult life — from civil rights, to labor activism, to talk radio — trying to convert the energy of a moment into the sustainability of a movement. Many of us have struggled for decades to maintain a momentum, to keep people focused, to not lose sight of the prize, in the midst of changing political winds, popular whims and bickering leadership.

I knew that for a moment to become a movement, there was one required element. Sacrifice.

So these young people had to do more than tweet a meme or join a message group. They had to put something at risk. Sure, they could go out and march, hold a few signs, then go back to their homes, their jobs, their campuses. But to do so in 2020, when a deadly virus literally was in the air around them, that would require a sacrifice. They had to put their lives on the line. To do so in 2021, when 30 million of them were instantly out of work because the economy had come to a screeching halt, that required sacrifice. And to do so when many in law enforcement were under orders to stop them with pepper spray, rubber bullets or worse, that required sacrifice.

Still, I worry. I feel mixed. I want to be optimistic. I want to believe that this is indeed a movement. But I am also fearful. I fear we are being set up. They may change some names, hire some Black folk, tear down some statues, but it may all just be window dressing. Real changes don't happen this quickly. I fear the okee-doke. That, just when we think there is real progress, then bam, they take it all away. I've seen it before. It could happen again.

But it was clear, this was their time. Us old-heads had our chance. We have accomplished a lot. We passed laws, transformed America, we even got a Black man elected president. But we still have a long way to go. We've run our leg of the marathon. We got the torch this far. Now it was time to light a younger generation's torch so it can finish the race.

Sitting in our home that evening, I knew I didn't need to be out on those streets with them, protesting and picketing, chanting and holding the bullhorn. Sherry was recovering from a stroke she had six months earlier, and I was battling a recurrence of prostate cancer.

For most of my life, I was out there, in the arena. I was doing something about it. And today, I am still in the arena, just using a different bullhorn. My place is on the air now, doing my radio show. Today, that is my bullhorn. That's where I can make my difference.

INDEX

2 Live Crew, 58
"60 Minutes," 54
Adams, Charles, 32
Adams, Yolanda, 90
AFL-CIO, 27
AIDS/HIV, 36, 82
Air America, 39
al-Bashir, Omar, 77-78
Ali, Khaliah, 82
Ali, Muhammad, 11, 82
American Anti-Slavery Group, 78
Amos, Robert, 12
Amos, Wally, Jr., 41
apartheid, 41-43
Apollo Theater, 127-128
Arlington National Cemetery, xiv
Armey, Dick, 73
Autry, Gene, 110
Banks, Doug, 90
Barry, Marion, 46
Battle, Buddy, 31
Before the Mayflower, 20
Benjamin, Rudy, 13
Bennett, Lerone, 20
Berry, Mary Frances, 117
Bethune-DuBois Institute, 59
Biden, Joseph, 41
Biggie (Notorious B.I.G.), 100
bin Laden, Osama, 99-100
Black Eagle, viii, x, xii-xiv
Black Entertainment Television, 123
Black Lives Matter, 46, 134
Black Panther Party, ix, x, 19
Bloomberg, Michael, 119
Bol, Manute, 75

Bond, Julian, 20, 90, 114, 127
Booker, Simeon, 20
Bottoms, Keisha Lance, 106
Bowman, Clarence, 8-9
Brown, Les, 47
Brown School of Social Work, 119
Brown, Sherrod, 41
Brown v. Board of Education, 34
Bunch, Lonnie, 115
Busey, Gary, 100
Bush, George W., 77, 92
Bush, Dorothy, 12
Byrd, Gary, 69
Caesars Palace, 41
Cain, Herman, 61
Caldwell, Jim, 13
Campbell, Luther, 58
Canton, Dave, vi, xi
Captain Kangaroo, 36
Carlin, George, 66, 129
Carlos, John, 84-85
Carnegie Hall, 122
"Celebrity Apprentice," 100
Central State University, Ohio, 14
Chauvin, Derek, 134
Chavis, Benjamin, 53-55
Cheadle, Don, 75
Cheney, Wayne, 46
Chicago Bears, 13
Christian Solidarity International, 3, 71, 72, 77
Chuck D, 39
CIA, 50-52, 76, 134
Civil War, 108
Clay, Cassius, 11

Clay, William, 52
Clear Channel, 70
Clinton, Bill, 55, 60, 73, 87, 92
Clinton, Hillary, 87, 101
Clooney, George, 75, 87
Clyburn, Jim, 127
CNN, 133
Coates, Laura, 120-121
Cochran, Father M.B., 16
Cochran, Johnnie, 30, 73-75
Cockrel, Ken, 30
Columbia University, 15, 98
Congressional Black Caucus, 50, 71, 73, 115-116, 127
Connecticut College, vi, viii
Contras, xii, 50
Conyers, John, 31-32
Cosby, Bill, 14, 41
COVID-19, 103-104
Cox, 39, 61
Crawford, Don, 13-14
Crawford, Donnella, 16-17
Cuba, xiv, 109, 115-118
Cumulus, 70
Cuomo, Andrew, 104, 106
Darfur, Sudan, ix, 75, 87
"Dark Alliance," 50
Davis, Joe, 32-33
Davis, Nate, 67
Dearborn, Michigan, boycott, 30-33
Death Row Records, 58
Democratic National Committee, 37
Democratic National Convention, 34, 50, 87
Detroit News, 33
Detroit Tigers, 35
diabetes, 79-82, 121
Dramatics, 29
Dr. Dre, 58
Duke, David, 101
Dukes, Ofield, 59
Dunbar High School, 13-14
Dunbar, Paul Laurence, 11, 14
Dwyer, Loretta B., 10-11
Dyson, Michael Eric, 69, 90, 95
Ebony, vi, 82
Edwards, Cid, 23
Elliott, Artie, 46-49, 76
Eminem, 58
Eve, 58

Evers, Medgar, 89-90
Evers-Williams, Myrlie, 55-56, 90-91
Famous Amos cookies, 41
Farrakhan, Louis, 37, 54, 78
Fauci, Anthony, 104
Faulkner, William, 14
Fauntroy, Walter, 48, 73-75
FBI, 49, 101
Featherstone, Art, 31, 33
Federal Communications Commission, 30, 66
Ferguson, Missouri, 47-48
Fifth Dimension, 24
"Finding Your Roots," 119, 123-126
Floyd, George, 134
Ford Foundation, 54
Ford, Henry, II, 31-32
Ford Motor Company, 30
Foreign Affairs Committee, 42
Four Tops, 16, 24, 109-110
Franken, Al, 39
Franklin, Aretha, 41, 113-114
Freedom Fund, 28-29, 32
gangster rap, 52, 58-59
Garang, John, 71
Garfield Elementary School, 14
Gates, Henry Louis "Skip," Jr., 119, 123-125
Gaye, Marvin, 109
General Motors, 65
George magazine, 64
George Washington Hospital, 120
Gianoulakis, Chris John, 25
Gibson, William, 53-54
Glover, Danny, 75
Goldberg, Whoopi, 110
Goldwater, Barry, 103
Goode, Wilson, 37
Gore, Al, 39
Graham, Donald, 65
Graham, Katharine, 65
Green, Al, 24
Green, Ernie, 16
Greene, Darrell, 104, 120
Greenstein, Scott, 129
Gregory, Dick, xii-xiii, 47, 50-52, 58, 109-114, 134
Gregory, Lillian, 111
Guerrero, Christopher Leon, 121
Guinness World Records, 29, 113-115

Haiti, 123
Hall, Elliott, 27
Hannity, Sean, 95
Hansberry, Lorraine, 14
Harris, Kamala, ix, 131
Hartmann, Thom, 76
Harvard University, 86-87, 98
Hayden, Leo, 13
Haygood, Herman, 125
Hemingway, Ernest, 14
Hemstreet, Mark, 83
HIV/AIDS, 36, 82
Holder, Eric, 106, 114
Hollywood Chamber of Commerce, 109, 111
Hollywood Walk of Fame, 109-111
Hooks, Benjamin, 30, 33, 41-42, 53, 127
Horne, Lena, 6
Horowitz, Michael, 73-74
House of Representatives, U.S., 102-103
Howard University, 17
Hudson Institute, 73
Hughes, Cathy, 47-48, 60-67, 69
Hughes, Langston, 14
Humphries, Rusty, 76
Hunter, Karen, 127
Hunter-Gault, Charlayne, 26
Image Awards, NAACP, 54-57
Imus, Don, 38
Interscope Records, 58
Iran-Contra affair, xii
Iraq war, 88
Jackson Elementary School, 8
Jackson, Jesse, 40-41, 43, 52-53, 82
Jackson, Jesse, Jr., 80-82
Jackson, Maynard, 80
Jackson, Samuel L., 62, 131
Jackson, Santita, 82
Jackson, Yvonne (Joe Madison's sister), 5, 7-8, 125
Jacobs, Charles, 78
Janjaweed militias, Sudan, 2
Jarrett, Valerie, 90, 93, 96
Jet, vi, 20, 82
Jim Crow, 108
Johnson, Arthur, 33
Johnson, Betty Lou, 5-7, 126
Johnson, Jack (boxer), 5
Johnson, Jack (prosecutor), 47-49
Johnson, Charles V., 42

Johnson, Orland, 22
Jones, Charlie, 45
Jones, Vivian, 26
Jordan, Vernon, 90
Joyner, Tom, 90
Julian, Hubert Fauntleroy, xiii-xiv
Just-Ice, 64
Karmazin, Mel, 68
Keith, Damon, 31, 33-34
Kemp, Brian, 106
Kennedy, John F. , Jr., 64
Kennedy, Robert, 64
Kesselring, Joseph, 14
"Key & Peele," 98
Keyes, Alan, 87-88
KFRH/KWUR, 22, 24
Kill the Messenger, 52
King, Albert, 29
King, Bob, 32, 34
King, Coretta Scott, 76
King, Martin Luther, III, 47
King, Martin Luther, Jr., ix, xiv, 19, 76, 89, 91, 96, 105, 112
King, Larry, 51
Kipling, Rudyard, 131
Knight, Suge, 58
LaVette, Bettye, 29, 114
Law, Bob, 69
League of Women Voters,106
Leavitt, Jason, 46
Legend, John, 111
Lewinsky, Monica, 73
Lewis, John, 73
Liggins, Alfred, III, 48, 62, 65, 67-69
Lil Jon, 100
Limbaugh, Rush, 38
Lincoln Center, 23
Lindbergh, Charles, xiii
Lisner Auditorium, 125
Little Richard, 56
Little Rock Nine, x, 16, 26
LL Cool J, 124
Lucas, Leo, 9
Madison, Felix, 5, 7, 124-126
Madison, Joe
 Activism, ix-x, 20-21, 30, 33, 35, 43, 88, 105, 126-127, 134
 Artie Elliott case, 46-49
 CIA/crack connection, 50-52

Hollywood Walk of Fame, 109-112
South Sudan, ix, 1-4, 71-78, 87
Voter registration, x, 40-41, 52, 87, 106, 123
Washington Post protest, 64-65
Ancestry, 5-7, 123-126
Early Life, 5-19
Education, 18-27
Football, 10, 13, 18-19, 21-26, 79
NAACP career, 27-44, 53-57, 87, 127
Radio career, viii-xiv, 22, 24, 34-39, 43-52, 60-70, 80, 83-84, 91-96, 101-108, 112-118, 122-123, 127-132
Madison, Sharon ("Sherry") LaVerne, vi, xiii, 1-4, 17-18, 67, 75-76, 92-94, 101, 120-122, 128, 130, 133, 135
"Madison Show," 112
Madonna, 64
Malcolm X, ix, 15
Marable, Manning (Billy), 15-16
Marac, Angelo, 3
Marquardt, Richard, 13, 18
Martin, Michel, 90
Martin, Richard, 25
Mathias, Charles, 42
McAdams, Butch, 61
McCain, Bernie, 60
McConnell, Mitch, 97
McLain, Denny, 35
McMillan, Ernie, 23
Mead Corporation, 27
Meat Loaf, 100
Medill School of Journalism, 17
Mfume, Kweisi, 75
Michigan Supreme Court, 32-33
Miller, Stephanie, 122
Milliken v. Bradley, 35, 39
Mirkin, Gabe, 79-80
Mitchell, Clarence, III, 61
Mitchell, Lisa, 61
Monroe, Bryan, vi, 82
Moore, Melba, 57-58
Morehouse College, 20, 22, 41, 60-61, 94, 130
"Morning Joe," 128-129
Motown, 16, 24, 29, 109
MSNBC, 128
Mt. Calvary Baptist Church, 15-16
Muhammad, Benjamin F., 54
Murphy, Eddie, 129

Murrow, Ed, 43
Muse, C. Anthony, 48
National Association for the Advancement of Colored People (NAACP), 27-30, 32, 34-35, 40-43, 49-50, 53-57, 62, 74, 87, 91, 127, 133
Nassau, Sam, 104
Nation of Islam, 37, 53-54, 78
National Action Network, 75
National Congress of Black Women, 57
National Enquirer, 94
National Geographic (TV), xiii
National Museum of African American History and Culture, 109, 113, 115, 123, 130
National Press Club, 87
NBC, 31, 60, 113, 128
Nelson, Willie, 39
New Bethel Baptist Church, 48
Newman, Sandy, 87
Nicaragua, 50
Nixon, Richard, 34, 103
North, Oliver, xii, xiv, 50-51
Northam, Ralph, 106
Northwestern University, 17
Nugent, John Peer, xiii
Obama, Barack, ix, 75, 83, 86-102, 104, 107, 115-116
Obama, Michelle, 94, 96, 99
O'Neal, Ron, 28
Overground Railroad, x, 40
Packer, Michael, 35
Parks, Rosa, ix, 31, 56, 105
Payne, Donald, 73
PBS, 125-126
Perez, Tom, 96
Pope, Alexander, 11
Port Gibson vs. NAACP, 29
Powell, Colin, 77-78
"Power, The," viii, 65
Procter & Gamble, 56
Project Vote, 87
prostate cancer, 83, 123, 125, 135
Pryor, Richard, 110, 129
Public Enemy, 39
Radio Hall of Fame, 119, 122-123
Radio One, 17, 47-48, 60, 63-70, 110
Ramsey, Jim, 41-42
Rangel, Charles, 73

Ratner, Ellen, 76
Raymond, Diane, 37
Reagan, Ronald, 43, 88, 99
Red Cross, 130
Renee, Shawna, vi, 17, 63-64, 96
Renner, Jeremy, 52
Republican Party, 39, 43, 75, 87, 93, 97-98, 101, 103, 106
Rice, Jack, 76
Rivera, Geraldo, 45-46, 76
Rivers, Jamie, 23
Robinson, Charlie, 21
Robinson, Smokey, 109
Rock, Chris, 112
Roker, Al, 81, 113
Romney, Mitt, 39, 103
Roosevelt, Franklin Delano, 107
Roosevelt High School, 10, 13-14
Roosevelt, Theodore, 10, 12, 14
Ross, "Freeway" Ricky, 50
Rowan, Carl, 29
Roweton, Sarah, 11
Rutgers University, 38
Ryan, April, 90
Samuels, Lynn, 66
San Jose Mercury News, 50
Sanders, Bernie, 101
Saperstein, David, 54
St. Louis Cardinals (football team), 22-23
St. Margaret's Episcopal Church, 15-16
Schmoke, Kurt, 62
Schwartz, Charles, 37
Scott, Mark, 34-35
Seagram, 58
Selassie, Haile, xiv
Selma (film), 52
Senate, U.S., 39, 42, 59, 87-88, 97-98, 103
Seymour Lundy, 27
Shakespeare, William, 12
Shakur, Tupac, 58, 100
Sharpton, Al, 38, 49, 52, 69, 75, 82-83, 90, 127, 133
Sheffield, Horace, Jr., 32
Shinhoster, Earl, 53
Siegelman, Don, 49-50
Simpson, Donnie, 122-123
Simpson, O.J., 74
Sirius Satellite Radio, 65

SiriusXM, x, 17, 65, 84, 99, 110, 112, 114-115, 123, 127-129, 131
Smith, Bev, 37-38
Smith, C. Miles, 60-63
Smith, H. Allen, xiv
Smith, Tommie, 85
Smithsonian, 88, 113, 115, 123, 130
South Africa, 31, 41-43
South Sudan/Sudan, ix, 1-4, 71-73, 75-79, 86-87, 92, 109, 123
Starr, Kenneth, 73-75
Stax Records, 16, 24
Steele, Michael, 75, 127
Stepp, Marc, 31
Stern, Howard, 38, 66, 129-130
Stone, Betty Lou, 5-7, 126
Stone, Jim, 5-6, 126
Stone, Nancy, 5-8, 14-15, 124-126
Student Nonviolent Coordinating Committee, x, 20, 52
Sudan Peace Act, 73
Supreme Court, U.S., 20, 29, 35, 103
Supremes, 109, 132
Talkers Magazine, 61, 76
Teigen, Chrissy, 111
Telecommunications Act of 1996, 60
Temptations, 16, 36, 109
Tennessee Valley Authority, 107
Thomas, Arthur, 14
Thompson, Benny, 127
Till, Emmett, 20
"Today Show," 31-33
Townsend, Kathleen Kennedy, 64
Trayvon Martin Foundation, 130
Trump, Donald, 98-108, 116, 131, 134
Tubman, Harriet, 40
Tucker, C. Delores, 57-59
Tucker, Chris, 111
Tuskegee Syphilis Study, 126
Underground Railroad, 40
UNICEF, 72
United Airlines, xiii, 17-18, 29
United Auto Workers, 31-32
University of Florida, vi, xi
University of Georgia, 26
USA Today, 115
Vietnam War, 11, 20, 108
Virgin Mary, 38
Voice of America, 17

WABC, 45, 66
Waldman, Suzyn, 122
Wallace, George, 47, 130
Wallace, Mike, 43
Walters, Ron, 73
Warwick, Dionne, 57-58
Washington, Harold, 86-87
Washington Hilton, 99
Washington Post, 64-65, 102, 108
Washington University, St. Louis,
    ix, 22-25, 27, 34, 119, 125
Watergate scandal, 134
Watergate Terrace, 23
Waters, Ethel, 6, 126
Waters, Maxine, 51, 127
WCHB, 35
Webb, Gary, 50, 52
WERQ-92, 17
WFAN, 122
Whitehead, Charles, 56
White House, 88-89, 91-93, 133-134
White House Correspondents Dinner, 99
Whitman, Walt, 14
Wickham, DeWayne, 115
Wicklin, Don, 93
Wilkerson, Lawrence, 77
Williams, Armstrong, 75-76
Williams, Hosea, 62
Winfrey, Oprah, ix, 114
Wisconsin State University,
    Whitewater, 18-19, 22
WOL-AM, 51, 60, 62-66, 69
WOLB-AM, 17, 60-61
Worldspace, 17
WPGC, 17
WRC/WWRC, xii, 17, 37-38,
    45-46, 50-51, 60, 63, 79
Wright, Jeremiah, 88
Wrighton, Mark, 119
WSB, 61
WWDB-FM, 36
WXYZ, 35
XM Satellite Radio, viii, 65-69
YMCA, 9
Young, Andrew, 62
Young, Coleman, 31, 33, 36
Young, Larry, 61

Made in the USA
Las Vegas, NV
16 March 2022